Guided Prayer Journal

# Call Me Wife

For Single Women Desiring Love and A Healthy Marriage

Dr. Dawn

*Hey God, it's me, Dawn. I listened! I poured myself into these pages. I pray that it touches every person you want it to touch.*

*Amen!*

# *Call Me, Wife*

# Content

| | |
|---|---|
| My Deepest Appreciation To……. | 5 |
| Preface: My Why AKA My Testimony | 7 |
| Introduction | 9 |
| *Part One: Shedding the Layers* | 11 |
| Day 1: Am I Called to Be a Wife? | 12 |
| Day 2: Who am I? | 20 |
| Day 3: What I am Leaving Behind? | 29 |
| Day 4: Who are You Worshiping? | 37 |
| Day 5: Hearing God's Voice | 43 |
| Day 6: Forgiving Yourself | 52 |
| Day 7: Forgiving Others | 63 |
| Day 8: Lessons and God's Rejection is Protection (The Hoodhealer, 2019) | 72 |
| Day 9: Imposter Syndrome | 79 |
| Day 10: Checking in With Your Real Desires | 86 |
| Day 11: Managing Expectations | 93 |
| Day 12: Making Room: Level of Conviction. | 101 |
| Day 13: Nourishing Your Soul | 110 |
| Day 14: Showing Gratitude | 119 |
| Day 15: Are You Who You Want to Marry? | 127 |
| Day 16: How Do I Want to Feel in My Marriage? | 135 |

| | |
|---|---|
| Day 17: My Ultimate Dream | 144 |
| *Part Two: Building the Wife* | 151 |
| Day 18: Limited Access | 152 |
| Day 19: While Single | 160 |
| Day 20: The Storms Within | 171 |
| Day 21: Divorcees | 180 |
| Day 22: Being the Virtuous Woman I am Assigned to Be | 189 |
| Day 23: Mothering My Children | 199 |
| Day 24: Biological Clock | 208 |
| Day 25: Waiting and Fasting | 216 |
| Day 26: Reflections of Love | 223 |
| *Part Three: I's almost married now!* | 232 |
| Day 27: Order and Submission | 233 |
| Day 28: Getting to the Aisle. | 242 |
| Day 29: A Prayer for The Wife I'm Called to Be | 252 |
| Day 30: A Prayer for My Husband | 260 |
| Day 31: Covering Our Union Now and Forever | 273 |
| Postscript | 282 |
| About the Author | 284 |
| References: | 285 |

# My Deepest Appreciation To.......

      I would like to express my deepest appreciation and gratitude to God first and then to my kids, Samuel, and Aniyah. Parenting you both has been the catalyst for my personal growth. I hope that this dedication serves as a reminder for you to always live and believe in yourselves, embracing your own journey, and learning from your mistakes. Above all, remember to prioritize your relationship with God.

      I would also like to extend my heartfelt thanks to my parents, Sherri and Olbin. Despite any hardships in their marriage, they demonstrate unwavering love for each other every day. They have taught me the true meaning of unconditional love and the importance of standing by someone's side as they evolve and discover themselves. They have also instilled in me the value of attending church and the power of prayer.

      To my mother, who has been both a mother and a best friend to me, I am incredibly grateful. Your presence and support have been invaluable throughout my life.

      My grandfather, Larry Sr., a pastor, holds a special place in my heart. He always made sure we were exposed to the church. Whenever we experienced the loss of a pet, he would deliver a heartfelt eulogy, reminding us of God's love.

      I cannot forget to thank my sister, Avianna. I am overjoyed to witness the amazing woman you are becoming. Your love for God inspires me, and I am grateful that my mom brought you into this world, as you have become my best friend.

      I want to express my appreciation to my brothers, Sadeil, Ladeil, and Kolbi. You taught me common behaviors of men. Whether near or far, you have all shown me immense support and love. I am truly blessed to have you in my life.

To my tribe, if you are in any group messages, or if I speak to you regularly. I love you - you motivate me and to my 6 God children. I love you real hard!!

Lastly, to my future husband, I've prayed for you since I was a little girl. I can't wait for you to meet my family and for me to meet yours. May God show us favor. I love you already!

# Preface: My Why AKA My Testimony

As I sit down to write my personal testimony, I am filled with a sense of vulnerability and courage. I feel compelled to share my journey of being single and the path that led me towards marriage. However, before drawing any conclusions, I want to clarify that I am not yet married. I have experienced divorce and am currently a single mother. Despite these circumstances, I have found peace and contentment in where I am, and I hope to encourage other women who may find themselves in similar situations. It is okay to be single for various reasons, such as: widowhood, divorce, or being a single mother. And even in singleness, it is still possible to desire a healthy and fulfilling marriage. You do have to know if God has called you to be married. If God has not told you this, close the book. Some of us are called to be single and serve. Single and serving does not equate to single and lonely. I've had many friends ask why haven't I made the book say partner, so it's inclusive and captivates a larger audience? This book isn't about inclusivity or sales. God revealed to me we need virtuous wives and faithful husbands in the world.

    The topics and journal prompts that I discuss may not resonate with everyone. This conversation can be polarizing and controversial because it challenges the traditional notion of wives appearing delicate or soft. We, as women, thrive in our independence and sometimes embrace masculinity as a means of feeling safe. This role allows us to shield ourselves from vulnerability, acting as a protective barrier against emotional harm. Yet, by embracing vulnerability and occasionally removing these barriers, we can hold men accountable, elevating the standards of faithfulness and responsibility. It is crucial to know our own worth and the level at which we operate. Are we strong, empowered women, willing to dismantle these barricades when necessary?

    I want to remind those who may feel discouraged or unworthy of finding love that they truly deserve a healthy and fulfilling relationship. You are worthy of this love, and settling for anything less is not an option. Through this journal, I hope to inspire and provide hope through guided prayers for those who may be struggling on their own journey towards love and companionship.

    As a woman with a background in mental health, I understand the difficulty of discussing singleness openly. However, through personal prayers and conversations with God, I have found peace and comfort on my journey. It is my desire to offer other women the same hope and strength that I have discovered.

    Sharing my personal prayers and conversations with God makes me feel vulnerable, but I believe in the importance of honesty and shedding the walls we build around ourselves. Some may perceive my unmarried status as a failure, but the truth is that I am exactly where God wants me to be, and I have found peace in that truth. Can I be honest? My ultimate goal, as I complete this journal, is to know my anointed, divine, capable, and God-fearing husband.

# Introduction

My intention is to empower women to embrace their personal journeys, whether they lead to marriage and love or to peace and contentment with the process. Through my personal testimony, I hope to instill strength and courage, encouraging women to trust in God's plan for their lives. This helps prepare us for when our husband finds us.

This book not only provides details of my personal journey towards love but also serves as a guide to empower women to embrace their own unique paths and find peace as they transition from being single to being married. As you read through these pages, remember that you are not alone. At every stage of your journey, hope and strength exist. While I write this book as Dr. Dawn Lewis, the author is simply Dr. Dawn, as my last name is pending. I am fully aware of my calling to be a wife, and I eagerly make room for the blessings that await.

**Biblical Scripture:** "For I know the plans I have for you," declares the Lord, "plans to prosper you and not to harm you, plans to give you hope and a future." - Jeremiah 29:11

This scripture serves as a reminder that God has a plan for our lives, and that plan includes our dreams and aspirations. When we partner with someone who shares our values and beliefs, we can work together to achieve our dreams and fulfill God's plan for our lives. By putting our faith in God and trusting His plan for our lives, we can have hope for the future and confidence that our dreams will come to fruition.

In bell hooks' book, "All about Love", she defines love as "the will to extend oneself for the purpose of nurturing one's own or another's spiritual growth." She emphasizes the importance of love as a practice, not just a feeling or emotion, and argues that it requires active effort and commitment to create and sustain healthy, loving relationships. Hooks also critiques mainstream cultural ideas about love, which often prioritize individualism, self-interest, and possession rather than the mutual care and growth that she believes are essential to true love.

I invite you to join me on this 31-day transformative journey. Embrace the challenges, uncertainties, and triumphs. Know that you are never alone and that there is strength and hope to be discovered in every stage. As we navigate the waters of singleness and marriage, let us trust in God's plan, embrace our vulnerabilities, and empower ourselves and one another. Together, we will find the love and companionship that we deserve.

As I reflect on my purpose and identity, I am reminded that God has a unique plan for my life. Through prayer and journaling, I hope to gain a deeper understanding of who I am in Christ and how I can fulfill His purpose for me. This guide will serve as a tool to help me grow in my faith and strengthen my relationship with God. I believe in the power of reading it, writing it, praying for it and professing it. Slowly this guide increases and encourages your journaling and prayer life. Being single is prep time, so let's go!

This guided prayer journal has a structure in which you will read my story, my prayers, complete the journal prompt, and write your own prayer. In my prayers, I may mention personal aspects such as being divorced and having children. I encourage you to read through topics you may feel are not applicable to you, as it still contains insightful information. Feel free to pause and digest as some prompts will take more time.

*Part One: Shedding the Layers*

*"The journey to wifely-hood, self-discovery, identity and worth requires an intimate relationship with God, discipline, dedication, and hard work"*
*~Dr. Dawn*

# Day 1: Am I Called to Be a Wife?

**Scripture:** "Wives, submit yourselves to your husbands, as is fitting in the Lord." - Colossians 3:18

The scripture advises wives to "submit" to their husbands. The term "submit" means to voluntarily place oneself under the authority or leadership of another. Here, it refers to wives willingly recognizing and respecting the role of their husbands as the head of the household.

The phrase "as is fitting in the Lord" adds a qualifier to this instruction. Submission is expected within the framework of beliefs and principles. It means that wives are called to submit to their husbands in a manner that aligns with the teachings of Jesus and the overall teachings of the Bible.

      This is the place where you want to start before proceeding with this book. You must know if you were called to be a wife. I've been single for almost 10 years. I really thought I was just going to be a mother, a woman who was able to travel once her kids left home and live a life of celibacy. Honestly, I was truly okay with this until November of last year. I had a dream of my husband, clear as day, and I woke up and prayed. I even told a couple of friends what he looked like. God revealed to me that I was indeed called to be a wife. Immediately, this shifted things, and I started making space for my future husband in my life, my mind, and even in my prayers. The minute you know you are called to be a wife; you have to assert a different level of discipline. You have to move in faith and remove those corrosive feelings of self-doubt, because once God tells you something, it's His word.

      My words, clothes, and lifestyle started mimicking how I want to be as a wife. I must admit, my presentation did differ from pre-calling. It wasn't a large gap, but it was small enough for me to recognize that a little bit of change had to take place. I even had to start talking to my children about opening their hearts for my husband/their bonus dad and possibly his children/their bonus siblings. We now all pray for him together as a family. Everyone must buy into the mission because they are a part of it. I had to reassure them that my love for them wouldn't change. I used this as a time to prepare their hearts and minds. This chapter is just to remind you that when you were called to be a wife, did you start showing up as one? So...when your husband finds you, there's no question, he just knows, and he moves accordingly.

Another big piece is being aware that you're submitting to his purpose and his purpose should ultimately be your purpose. What you will see is that God will align what you've been doing in life with the overall purpose. Are you prepared for this level of submission? I am an independent woman, so I had to envision what that looks like and prepare myself for submitting to that. And honestly, when I think of it, I smile. I'm ready. Not only do I know what it takes, but I'm ready to live in that. As you move forward, you will see what deepening this commitment means and looks like without losing yourself, which many of us fear when we hear biblical terminology.

**Journal Prompt:** Am I Called to Be a Wife?

- How do you understand the idea of submission in the context of marriage? What are your initial thoughts and feelings about it?

- Have you ever felt a calling or sense that you are meant to be a wife? If so, how did that realization impact your perspective on submission?

- In what ways have you started making space for your future husband in your life, mind, and prayers? How has this process of preparation and mindset shift been for you?

- How do you reconcile being an independent woman with the idea of submitting to your husband's purpose? How can you envision this submission as a partnership rather than a loss of yourself?

  - **Important** Remember, as you deepen your readings in this guide, you will have the ability to discern everything from God's voice to ungodly thoughts.

*Journal here*

**Prayer Prompt:** Am I Called to Be a Wife?

Dear Heavenly Father,

  Thank You for the guidance and wisdom found in your Word. As I reflect on the concept of submission in marriage, I come to You with an open heart and a willingness to understand your will for my life. Help me to navigate this topic with humility, grace, and a deep sense of love for You and my future husband.

  I recognize that submission is not about diminishing my worth or losing my identity, but about embracing the role You have called me to as a wife. Give me the strength and courage to align my thoughts, words, and actions with this calling. Show me how to make space in my life, mind, and prayers for my future husband, preparing myself to fully embrace the partnership of marriage.

  Help me to see submission as a beautiful collaboration between my husband and I, where we both seek to fulfill your purpose for our lives. Give me the wisdom to discern a husband who is devoted to You, who leads with love and humility. Guide my husband on his journey of finding me that he will cherish and respect me, just as I will cherish and respect him.

  Lord, I pray for the ability to maintain my individuality and personal goals while honoring my role as a wife. Help me to find a balance where I can support my husband's purpose while pursuing my own passions and dreams. Teach me how to submit without losing myself, but rather to grow and flourish within the context of a loving and God-centered marriage.

  Thank You, Lord, for your guidance and presence in my life. May your love and grace shine through my actions and decisions as I seek to understand and live out the concept of submission in marriage.

  In Jesus' name, I pray.

  Amen.

*My Prayer....*

# Day 2: Who am I?

**Scripture:** "I know that you can do all things; no purpose of yours can be thwarted." - Job 42:2

    I am a woman of strong faith, a proud black woman who finds joy in helping and listening to others. I cherish the bonds of friendship and am known for my unwavering loyalty and infectious laughter. With few regrets, I have worked hard to provide for my children and have a heart full of love to share with the right partner. My values guide me through life, and I am grateful for all that my life has to offer. I am a caring and loving person, with a big heart and a desire for companionship and partnership. In essence, I am a healthy, grateful, and appreciative woman who knows what she wants in life.

    I am also an avid traveler. Traveling allows my soul to connect with others and blossom. I believe that we are all interconnected, and I love to explore different cultures and communities to learn from them. Traveling has also taught me the value of living in the moment and appreciating the beauty of the present. It has helped me cultivate a sense of gratitude and humility, knowing that there is so much more to life than what I experience in my daily routine. If given the chance, I would save the world, and it is my goal to do so; preferably with my soulmate by my side. Together, we can make a positive impact on the world and leave a lasting legacy that we can be proud of.

    My heart is filled with a deep desire to break the cycle of generational trauma and burdens that have been inherited by my family. It is a motivator that drives me to push forward every day. My faith and personal experiences have all played a significant role in my journey towards healing. I feel a strong obligation to pursue this mission with the support of God, leading by example and organizing therapeutic retreats. It is my sincerest desire to offer a range of different modalities that can help others find their path towards healing and relief, and to do so with compassion and empathy. I believe that by healing these wounds, our future generations can live a life free from the weight of past struggles. I want our children to have the freedom to make mistakes and live in peace without the fear of carrying the same burdens as their ancestors. It is my hope that by breaking the cycle of trauma, we can create a better future for all.

  When embarking on a journey towards marriage, it's essential to take a moment to reflect on who you truly are. I urge you to look beyond the titles and achievements that define your professional life. Instead, take a deep dive into your values, your personality, and the way you present yourself to others. These are the qualities that truly matter in a relationship. Remember, a true God-fearing and faithful man's relationship with God is one rooted in love, trust, and devotion. Such a man recognizes the importance of having a personal connection with God and seeks to strengthen it through prayer, worship, and studying sacred texts.

  A man who fears God and remains faithful to Him strives to live according to God's teachings and principles in his daily life. He seeks to align his actions, thoughts, and intentions with what he believes to be God's will. This may include treating others with kindness, compassion, and respect, as well as practicing forgiveness and seeking reconciliation when conflicts arise.

  A faithful man often finds council and guidance in times of difficulty or uncertainty by turning to God for support. He leans on his faith to find comfort, strength, and hope, and he believes that God's presence is with him in every aspect of life. This relationship with God brings him peace, joy, and a sense of purpose.

It's important to remember that everyone's relationship with God is unique, and each person's life will look different. However, a God-fearing and faithful man is someone who embraces a spiritual journey with God, seeks to live a life of integrity and righteousness, and continually strives to deepen his connection with God. So, take a moment to reflect on who you are, and let your true self shine in your journey towards marriage.

**Journal Prompt:** Who am I?

- Who am I and what am I trying to achieve with this prayer guided journal?

- As a single woman, what are some areas in my life that I can focus on to prepare for marriage?

- How can I use this journal to guide me during this process?

*Journal here*

**Prayer Prompt**: Who am I?

Dear God,

Please guide me as I prepare my heart and life for marriage. Help me to trust in your timing and plan, and to use this prayer guided journal as a tool to grow closer to you and become the best version of myself.

Amen.

*My Prayer....*

# Day 3: What I am Leaving Behind?

**Scripture:** "For this reason, a man will leave his father and mother and be united to his wife, and the two will become one flesh." - Genesis 2:24

    As I reflect on the things, I am leaving behind in order to pursue marriage, I am aware of the sacrifices I am making. I am letting go of my fear of vulnerability and opening myself up to the possibility of being hurt. I am leaving behind my desire for complete independence and embracing the idea of sharing my life with someone else. I am sacrificing my comfort zone and stepping into the unknown.

    Are these sacrifices worth it? Absolutely. While it may be challenging to leave behind these familiar aspects of my life, I believe that the rewards of a loving and fulfilling marriage are far greater. The joy of companionship, the support and encouragement, the shared dreams and goals; these are the treasures that make the sacrifices worthwhile.

    Leaving these things behind is not easy, but I am determined to grow and evolve as a person. I recognize that negativity, fear, and self-reliance will only hinder my ability to form a strong and healthy relationship. By letting go of these negative patterns, I am creating space for love, trust, and vulnerability to flourish.

    I felt a mix of emotions about leaving these things behind. There is a sense of excitement and anticipation for what lies ahead, as I know that a loving partnership adds immense joy and fulfillment. At the same time, there is a tinge of sadness and apprehension, as I am stepping into the unknown and leaving behind what is familiar to me. This doesn't mean I lack faith.

However, I am committed to embracing this journey of growth and transformation. I trust that God has a plan for me, and He will guide me through this process of letting go and stepping into a new chapter of my life. I know that His love and grace will sustain me, and that the sacrifices I am making are ultimately for my own well-being and happiness.

I am willingly leaving behind negative thoughts, past experiences, and making sacrifices in order to pursue a healthy marriage. I believe these sacrifices are worth it, as they pave the way for a God led, fulfilling and loving relationship. Though it may be difficult to leave these things behind, I trust in God's guidance and look forward to the blessings that await me on this journey.

**Journal Prompt**: What I am Leaving Behind?

Reflect on the things you are leaving behind in order to pursue marriage.

- o What are the sacrifices you are making? Are these sacrifices worth it? How do you feel about leaving these things behind?

*Journal here*

**Prayer Prompt:** What I am Leaving Behind?

Dear God,

    I come before You with a heart that longs for Godly love and companionship. I am leaving behind patterns and relationships that no longer serve me, and I am trusting you to guide me towards a healthy and fulfilling marriage.

    Lord, I pray that You help me to let go of any negative patterns or beliefs that have been passed down through generations before me. I pray that You break any generational curses that may hinder me from experiencing the love and joy that You have in store for me.

    As I embark on this journey, I ask that You keep me grounded in your love and your truth. Help me to keep You at the forefront of my mind, so that I may make wise choices and honor You in all that I do.

    Finally, Lord, I pray that You prepare my heart and the heart of my future husband for the love that you have planned for us. May we both be ready and open to receive the love that You have in store for us, and may we use our love to honor and glorify You.

Amen.

*My Prayer....*

# Day 4: Who are You Worshiping?

**Scripture:** "You will seek Me and find Me when you seek Me with all your heart." - Jeremiah 29:13:

This scripture supports the idea of relying on God and developing a deep relationship with Him rather than relying on external tools. It emphasizes the importance of a genuine, personal relationship with Him. This verse reminds us that when we wholeheartedly seek God, we will find Him.

In today's world, it's easy to become absorbed in the things that society has presented to us as valuable and entertaining. However, it's important to reflect on who or what we are truly devoting our time and energy to. I understand that this topic may be difficult for some, but it's worth considering. There was a time when I personally relied on tools like crystals, chakras, and oracle cards to find guidance and support. But as I grew spiritually, I realized that my ultimate source of strength and wisdom comes from God. He provides us with tools. The most powerful tool is prayer and developing a deep relationship with Him.

Divination served as a temporary remedy when I felt lost or uncertain, but now that I am more faithful and dedicated to prayer, I no longer feel the need for them. I believe that by relying on these external tools, we may unintentionally dilute our connection with God and limit our true spiritual experience. Instead, I encourage you to take a moment to truly meditate and connect with God on a personal level. When we have a genuine relationship with Him, we will find that the need for such tools diminishes.

**Journal Prompt:** Who are You Worshiping?

Reflect on your own spiritual journey and the tools or practices you have relied on for guidance and support.

- Have you ever found yourself relying more on divination rather than developing a deep relationship with God?

- How has this impacted your spiritual experience? What steps can you take to strengthen your connection with God and rely on Him solely?

*Journal here*

**Prayer prompt:** Who are You Worshiping?

Lord,

I come before You today humbly and sincerely. I acknowledge that at times, I have relied on external tools and practices for guidance and support, rather than developing a deep relationship with You. I confess that this has impacted my spiritual experience, sometimes diluting my connection with You.

But today, I desire to change that. I want to seek You with all my heart, as your word promises that when I do, I will find You. Help me to let go of any reliance on divination that may hinder my relationship with You. Open my eyes to the power of prayer and the importance of developing a genuine, personal connection with You.

Guide me in taking the necessary steps to strengthen my connection with You. Help me to prioritize spending time in prayer, meditation, seeking your wisdom and guidance. Teach me to rely on your presence and your word as my ultimate source of strength and direction.

Lord, I surrender any reliance on worldly practices and practices that are not of You. Fill me with your Holy Spirit and draw me closer to You each day. May my relationship with You deepen and flourish, so that I may experience the fullness of your love and purpose for my life.

In Jesus' name, I pray.

Amen.

*My Prayer....*

# Day 5: Hearing God's Voice

**Scripture:** "No temptation has overtaken you except what is common to mankind. And God is faithful; He will not let you be tempted beyond what you can bear. But when you are tempted, He will also provide a way out so that you can endure it."- 1 Corinthians 10:13

This scripture reminds us that God understands our struggles and temptations, and He will always provide a way for us to resist and overcome them. It's encouraging to know that you have been actively seeking His guidance and staying strong in your convictions.
Remember to continue relying on God's wisdom and strength as you navigate this situation. He will lead you towards the higher purpose He has for your life.

    I met a man, and he seemed perfect on paper. He was on a journey, very self-aware, but operating in his flesh. The tension between us was so strong that you could almost cut through it with a machete. We avoided temptation despite our strong physical connection. He said I was not his wife since he had a sexual desire for me initially. I disagreed then and I still do now. I understood that although we may experience lust, we don't have to entertain that temptation. I deliberately avoided being alone with him since I knew how frail our flesh was. I didn't want to take the possibility of compromising my chances of becoming his wife by caving in to fleeting pleasure. Thus, I prayed for deliverance.
    Every time I am in his presence, I still feel that he has a higher purpose in my life. I heard God's voice urging me to leave him be and stay still until He tells me to move. This was a difficult decision, but I chose to listen. Although

he had the language to articulate a healthy relationship, he lacked the sophistication to execute it. It takes a certain level of inner awareness and deliverance to hear God's voice. Thankfully, God met me where I was at and spoke to me clearly. He advised me not to sleep with this man because we both have a higher purpose in this life together. And I listened.

This clear message from God was made possible due to my level of atonement in my spiritual ascension. I have worked on strengthening my communication with God through continual prayer, fasting, sitting with His word, and building a relationship with Him. This ongoing practice has allowed me to grow in my relationship with Christ and minimize any confusion between my voice and God's voice. Discerning God's voice can be increasingly difficult if you haven't spent time with Him. If your degree of discernment is weak, you may misconstrue God's voice for either your own or the devil's. Growing up, my pastor taught me that we should not pray to become righteous, but rather, we should pray because that is what righteous people do. It's a beautiful perspective that reminds us of the importance of connecting with God through prayer and seeking His guidance.

Currently, the man mentioned, and I are attempting a business opportunity together with no blurred lines. I am grateful for the strength and guidance I have received. It has allowed me to navigate this situation while staying true to my spiritual journey.

**Journal Prompt:** Hearing God's Voice

Reflect on a time when you had to discern God's voice amidst the noise of the world. Write about the process you went through to discern His voice and how you knew it was truly Him speaking to you.

- What factors helped you differentiate between God's voice, your own desires, or the opinions of others?

- How did you feel when you realized it was God's voice guiding you? How did this experience deepen your trust and reliance on Him?

- Explore any challenges or doubts you faced during the discernment process and how you overcame them.

Reflect on the impact of hearing and following God's voice in your life and how it has shaped your journey.

*Journal here*

**Prayer Prompt:** Hearing God's Voice

Heavenly Father,

    Thank You for being a God who speaks to His children. You know the struggles and temptations we face, and You promise to provide a way out. I come before You today to seek your guidance and discern your voice amidst the noise of the world.

    As I reflect on a time when I had to discern your voice, I am reminded of the challenges and doubts I faced. There were moments when my own desires and the opinions of others clouded my judgment. But in those moments, You gave me a deep inner knowing, a sense of peace and clarity, that could only come from You.

    Thank You for the factors that helped me differentiate your voice from my own desires. It was through prayer, spending time with You, and immersing myself in your Word that I could align my thoughts and desires with your will. Your voice resonates with truth, love, and a higher purpose that goes beyond temporary satisfaction.

    When I realized it was your voice guiding me, I felt a profound sense of awe and gratitude. Knowing that the Creator of the universe was speaking directly to me, filled me with humility and reverence. It deepened my trust and reliance on You, knowing that your guidance is always for my ultimate good.

    Lord, I acknowledge the challenges and doubts I faced during the discernment process. There were moments when I questioned whether it was truly You speaking or just my own thoughts. But through prayer and surrender, You quieted the doubts and affirmed your presence in my life.

    I am immensely grateful for the impact of hearing and following your voice in my life. It has shaped my journey and has led towards a deeper relationship with You and a greater understanding of your purpose for me. Help me to continue seeking your guidance and discerning your voice amidst the noise of the world. May your voice always be my guiding light, leading me on the path of righteousness.

    In Jesus' name, I pray.

    Amen.

*My Prayer....*

# Day 6: Forgiving Yourself

**Scripture:** "If we confess our sins, He is faithful and just and will forgive us our sins and purify us from all unrighteousness." - John 1:9

This verse reminds us that when we confess our sins and seek forgiveness from God, He is faithful to forgive us and cleanse us from all unrighteousness. It emphasizes the importance of acknowledging our mistakes, seeking forgiveness, and allowing God's grace to restore us. By forgiving ourselves, we align ourselves with God's forgiveness and open ourselves to healing and growth.

Forgiving yourself is vital for preparing for your husband because when he finds you, you don't want to be in a place of trauma or lack. Now, we all have our own baggage, and no one is ever completely healed. Even so, be mindful to extend yourself forgiveness.

I've heard from several of my friends, "Dawn, you're so balanced," and I know it's because I've learned to forgive myself. I don't beat up on myself for the things of the past or mistakes I'll make.

I learned the art of forgiveness by knowing what I'm not willing to accept. I met a man who had a great job, believed in God-ish (which should've been a dealbreaker), didn't have kids, and had never been married. We spoke for a while and discovered that we had many similar interests. It was so beautiful because we met in Paris, just to find out that we lived 6 miles away from each other in Atlanta. After talking, I really liked him. A couple months in, I told him a lie, that not only caused him to not trust me, but it also created somewhat of a rift between us.

We continued to talk and even traveled to see one another when we were in different states. I could feel that he was trying to get to know me, but there was this level of resistance. I asked him what it was, and he told me that not only was it the lie I told, understandably, but he wasn't excited about being a stepdad. This was new information. To confirm that what I heard him say was correct, I asked him about it once again. Once he confirmed it, I was okay with ending the situation because, as much as I desire to be a wife, any man that finds me must be excited about being a bonus dad and a lifelong mentor to my children.

    In order to forgive myself and move on, one of the monumental things that I did was lay flat on my face and cry. I didn't trust the signs God had provided me. I cried for allowing myself to talk to someone and not be aware of the signs. The emotional purge was so refreshing. I then prayed and asked God to equip me. I asked Him to allow me to become familiar with certain behaviors and words that aren't in alignment with His will. I promised myself that I will never allow someone who is still questioning their relationship with God or lacks the ability to communicate their dealbreakers (e.g., not interested in children) in my life. I fasted, I prayed, I watched sermons, and I exercised to reduce the stress of letting go. I felt like I covered all of my bases. It wasn't overnight, but once I realized that God's rejection was protection (Hoodhealer, 2019), I felt the wounds close, almost instantaneously.

    Many women have previous partners that they absolutely regret. I encourage you to remove that energy from your space and your body by forgiving yourself. Feelings of regret and unforgiveness will show up and manifest in your marriage if you don't allow yourself to heal from them. The reality is, we all have a past, and we all have things that we aren't proud of, but there's no need to carry them into something that is meant to be holy. Clear that space within you to make room for your husband. Other than your relationship with God, your marriage is sacred, so prepare for it as though it's such. Remember, your past has made you the woman you are today. Embrace your journey and allow it to strengthen your relationship with Christ.

**Journal Prompt:** Forgiving Yourself

Reflect on the things from your past that you haven't fully forgiven yourself for.

- Write down those experiences or mistakes that still weigh on your heart and mind. Allow yourself to feel the emotions associated with them, but also remind yourself that you are worthy of forgiveness and healing.

- Next, write a letter of forgiveness to yourself. Address it to your past self, expressing compassion, understanding, and forgiveness for the mistakes or regrets you carry. Acknowledge that you are a different person now. You are someone who is capable of growth and change.

- In the letter, affirm your commitment to let go of any negative energy or self-blame associated with those past experiences. Embrace the lessons learned and the growth that has come from them. Declare that you are ready to open yourself up to love, joy, and a healthy relationship.

- Finish the journal entry by writing down affirmations that reinforce self-forgiveness and the preparation for a sacred marriage. For example, "I forgive myself for the past and embrace my journey of growth and healing. I am worthy of love and a healthy marriage. I am open and ready to welcome my future husband with a healed heart."

Recall, the process of forgiving oneself takes time and self-compassion. Be patient with yourself and trust that by letting go of the past, you are creating space for a beautiful future.

*Journal here*

**Prayer Prompt:** Forgiving Yourself

Heavenly Father,

I come before You with a humble and contrite heart, seeking your forgiveness and grace. I acknowledge my sins and mistakes, and I ask for your mercy and cleansing. Thank You for the promise in John 1:9, that if we confess our sins, You are faithful and just to forgive us and purify us from all unrighteousness.

 Lord, I ask for your help in forgiving myself for the things from my past that still burden me. I release the guilt, shame, and regret that I have carried, and I surrender them to You. Please fill me with your love and compassion, reminding me of my worthiness of forgiveness and healing.

 I pray for the strength and courage to let go of any negative energy or self-blame associated with my past experiences. Help me to embrace the lessons learned and the growth that has come from them. Guide me in opening myself up to love, joy, and a healthy marriage. Prepare my heart, mind, and spirit for a sacred union with my future husband.

 Lord, I surrender my desires and expectations to You. I trust that You have a plan for my life and that You will bring the right husband into my life at the right time. Help me to align my desires with your will and be blessed with a husband who shares my values and is excited about being a bonus dad and a lifelong mentor to my children.

 Thank You, Lord, for your forgiveness, your grace, and your guidance. I surrender myself to You. I know that through embracing my journey and allowing it to strengthen my relationship with You, I will be prepared for the sacred marriage You have planned for me.

 Amen.

*My Prayer....*

# Day 7: Forgiving Others

**Scripture:** "For if you forgive others their trespasses, your heavenly Father will also forgive you, but if you do not forgive others their trespasses, neither will your Father forgive your trespasses." - Matthew 6:14-15

"Do not judge, and you will not be judged. Do not condemn, and you will not be condemned. Forgive, and you will be forgiven."- Luke 6:37

These scriptures remind us of the importance of forgiveness and how God's forgiveness serves as a model for us. By forgiving others, we not only free ourselves from the burden of resentment, but also reflect God's love and mercy.
Forgiving oneself is a prerequisite to forgiving others and it is also a transformative catalyst for sanctification and leading a life free from offense. Forgiveness is a complex concept that can be challenging for many people to understand. Personally, I thrive in forgiveness and have encountered numerous situations where I had to activate my forgiveness switch. I've come to realize that forgiveness is not necessarily for the benefit of the person being forgiven, but rather for my own growth and well-being. By forgiving others, I create space for new opportunities and positive experiences to flourish in my life.
Recently, my mother reminded me of the various layers of forgiveness I have experienced throughout my life. Although I haven't forgotten the past incidents, I have utilized them as part of my testimony. I have been able to generate healing and expansion in my life through genuine forgiveness.

For instance, I am the product of a marriage marred by abuse. My father, who was young and struggling with substance abuse, tragically died of AIDS in 1992. He was only 29 years old. As I approached the age of 29 myself, I couldn't help but fear that I might suffer the same fate, even though I had led a responsible lifestyle. I vividly remember the days when my father was quarantined due to the limited understanding of how AIDS was spread. He confided in my mother that he couldn't feel his fingertips as his body deteriorated. At the tender age of seven, I had fleeting thoughts that he deserved this fate for abandoning his children due to his selfish actions.

However, instead of allowing anger and resentment to consume me, I made the conscious decision to forgive him. This act of forgiveness empowered me to truly understand who he was as a person. I now share the positive memories I have of him with my own children, without shame or judgment. I use these stories to teach them about the destructive power that worldly temptations and vices can have on one's life. Forgiving my father has been a source of strength and has allowed me to reclaim years of my life that would have otherwise been lost to bitterness and anger.

Witnessing my mother gracefully navigate her own marriage and life, despite the challenges she faced, has further emphasized the power of forgiveness. She, too, has forgiven my father and has been blessed by God through her children. It is incredible to see how forgiving others can break the chains of stagnation and open the door to blessings and growth.

I urge you to embrace forgiveness wholeheartedly, no matter the cost. Forgiveness is a transformative force that can restore peace and happiness in your life. Let go of grudges, resentments, and allow forgiveness to set you free.

**Journal Prompt:** Forgiving Others

Reflect on a time when you struggled to forgive someone.

- What were the reasons behind your resistance to forgive? How did holding onto resentment affect your well-being? Consider any grudges or resentments you may be holding onto. How do these negative emotions impact your daily life and relationships? What steps can you take to release these grudges and embrace forgiveness?

- Have you ever experienced the transformative power of forgiveness in your life? Describe a situation where forgiveness brought healing and growth. Think about someone you may need to forgive currently. What steps can you take to cultivate forgiveness towards that person? How might forgiving them benefit your own growth and well-being?

Reflect on the scriptures mentioned earlier about forgiveness.

- How do these verses speak to you personally? How can you apply the teachings of forgiveness in your own life?

- Write about a time when you received forgiveness from someone. How did their act of forgiveness impact you? How can you extend that same grace and forgiveness to others?

*Journal here*

**Prayer Prompt:** Forgiving Others

Dear Heavenly Father,

    I come before You today, grateful for your love and mercy, and for the power of forgiveness that You have shown us through your teachings. Your word reminds me that if I forgive others of their trespasses, You will also forgive me. Help me to understand the depth and importance of forgiveness in my life.

    Lord, I confess that there have been times when I have struggled to forgive. The reasons behind my resistance were fear, hurt, and a desire for justice. But holding onto resentment only weighed me down and affected my well-being. It hindered my ability to experience true peace and joy. I ask for your guidance and strength to release these grudges and resentments that I am holding onto. Help me to embrace forgiveness and let go of the burdens that are weighing me down.

    I acknowledge that forgiveness is not always easy, but I have witnessed its transformative power in my life. There was a situation where forgiveness brought healing and growth. Through your grace, I was able to forgive and let go of the pain that was holding me captive. It allowed me to move forward and experience freedom and peace. Thank You for showing me the power of forgiveness and for the growth it has brought into my life.

    Lord, I recognize that there may be someone in my life whom I need to forgive currently. I pray for the strength and wisdom to cultivate forgiveness towards that person. Help me to see them with compassion and understanding, just as You see me. I know that forgiving them will benefit my own growth and well-being. Give me the courage to extend forgiveness and to release any bitterness or anger that I may be holding onto.

As I reflect on the scriptures about forgiveness, they speak to my heart. Your words remind me of your boundless love and mercy, and they challenge me to live a life free from judgment and condemnation. I pray for the grace to apply these teachings of forgiveness in my own life. Help me to forgive others as You have forgiven me and to reflect your love and mercy to those around me.

Lord, I am grateful for the times when I have received forgiveness from others. Their act of forgiveness impacted me deeply and allowed me to experience your grace in a tangible way. Help me to extend that same grace and forgiveness to others. Teach me to let go of any resentment or judgment and to offer forgiveness freely, just as You have forgiven me.

I thank You, Lord, for the transformative power of forgiveness. I pray for the strength and courage to embrace forgiveness wholeheartedly, no matter the cost. Help me to let go of grudges and resentments. I ask to experience the restoration, peace, and happiness that forgiveness brings. May forgiveness set me free to live a life that reflects your love and mercy.

In Jesus' name, I pray.

Amen.

*My Prayer....*

# Day 8: Lessons and God's Rejection is Protection (The Hoodhealer, 2019)

**Scripture:** "And we know that in all things God works for the good of those who love Him, who have been called according to his purpose." -Romans 8:28 (NIV)

This verse reminds us that God can work all things, including rejections, for our ultimate good and according to His purpose in our lives.

In life, we often find ourselves questioning the reasons behind the end of a relationship. We wonder what we did wrong or why things didn't work out as we hoped. But let me offer you a perspective that is both inspirational and godly: sometimes, God's rejection is actually His way of protecting us.

When we encounter relationships that don't align with our values or where the other person's life is not in order, it's essential to recognize these as lessons. We learn from these experiences, gaining a deeper understanding of what it truly means to be with a God-fearing individual. This understanding becomes a guiding light, leading us towards finding a partner whose life is a true reflection of their relationship with God.

In these moments of questioning, remember that God has a plan for each one of us. He sees what we cannot, and sometimes the end of a relationship is His way of redirecting us towards something better. So, let us embrace these life lessons and trust that God's rejection is ultimately His way of protecting us and leading us to a more fulfilling and God-centered marriage.

**Journal Prompt:** Lessons and God's Rejection is Protection (The Hoodhealer, 2019)

Reflect on a time when you experienced rejection in a relationship or a similar situation.

- How did you initially feel and how did it impact your perspective on the situation? Did you eventually come to see it as God's way of protecting you? If so, how did that realization bring you comfort or guidance? If not, what prevented you from seeing it in that light?

- How can you trust in God's plan and His protection in future situations of rejection?

*Journal here*

**Prayer Prompt:** Lessons and God's Rejection is Protection (The Hoodhealer, 2019)

Dear Heavenly Father,

     In moments of questioning and confusion, help me to understand the lessons You have for me in the midst of rejection. Open my heart and mind to the wisdom and growth that can come from these experiences. Show me how to learn from them and gain a deeper understanding of your will for my life.

     Grant me the clarity to see beyond my initial emotions and perspective. Help me to recognize your hand at work, guiding and protecting me through the rejection. Give me the strength to trust in your plan, even when it may be difficult to understand.

     As I reflect on past rejections, help me to see them as opportunities for growth and redirection. Reveal to me the ways in which You were protecting me and leading me towards a more fulfilling and God-centered path. Fill me with comfort and guidance as I come to realize your loving hand in those situations.

     In future moments of rejection, give me the faith and discernment to see them as your way of protecting me and leading me towards something better. Help me to trust in your plan and your protection; knowing that You work all things for my ultimate good.

     In Jesus' name,

     Amen.

*My Prayer....*

# Day 9: Imposter Syndrome

**Scripture:** "All who make idols are nothing, and the things they treasure are worthless. Those who would speak up for them are blind; they are ignorant, to their own shame. Who shapes a god and casts an idol, which can profit nothing?" - Isaiah 44:9-10

This passage emphasizes the emptiness and worthlessness of idols, highlighting the foolishness of placing our trust and admiration in something or someone other than God. It reminds us that these false idols have no power or ability to bring true value or fulfillment into our lives. Instead, our focus should be on the one true God who alone is worthy of our worship and devotion.

Imposter syndrome is a common experience that many people face. One of the main aspects of this syndrome is getting caught up in comparison mode. It is crucial to resist the temptation of comparing ourselves to unrealistic #RelationshipGoals or false celebrity idols. We often know nothing about the reality of their relationships behind closed doors. It is easy to get caught up in this mindset, especially when there are countless self-proclaimed experts offering their opinions. However, it is important to be cautious about who we listen to and to not let others define who we are or how we should show up. Instead, let's be our own relationship goals and strive to be the best version of ourselves. This applies not only to personal relationships but also to work relationships and our marriages. It is vital to protect and nurture these connections at all costs.

**Journal Prompt:** Imposter Syndrome

Reflect on a time when you have felt the pressure to compare yourself or your relationships to false idols or unrealistic standards.

- How did this impact your self-esteem and overall well-being?

- How can you shift your focus away from these false idols and instead prioritize your own growth, authenticity, and the values that truly matter to you?

- How can you create a healthy mindset that allows you to appreciate and nurture your own unique relationships, rather than striving to meet external expectations?

*Journal here*

**Prayer Prompt:** Imposter Syndrome

Dear God,

Thank You for reminding me through your word that idols are empty and worthless. Help me to resist the temptation to compare myself and my relationships to false idols and unrealistic standards. I acknowledge that these comparisons only lead to feelings of inadequacy and diminish my self-esteem.

Instead, I pray that You would guide me to focus on my own growth, authenticity, and the values that truly matter to me. Help me to cultivate a healthy mindset that allows me to appreciate and nurture my own unique relationships, rather than striving to meet external expectations.

Please, grant me the wisdom to discern who I should listen to and not let others define who I am or how I should show up in my relationships. Help me to achieve my own marriage goals, striving to be the best version of myself.

Thank You for the reminder that You alone are worthy of my worship and devotion. May my heart always be centered on You and your truth.

In Jesus' name, I pray.

Amen.

*My Prayer....*

# Day 10: Checking in With Your Real Desires

**Scripture:** "Search me, O God, and know my heart! Try me and know my thoughts! And see if there be any grievous way in me, and lead me in the way everlasting!" - Psalm 139:23-24

This passage is a prayer for God to search our hearts, examine our thoughts, and reveal any areas that need correction or alignment with His will. It expresses a desire to be led by God on the everlasting path of righteousness and truth. Reflecting on your journey towards embracing marriage and acknowledging your true desires can align with the idea of trusting in God's plan and seeking His guidance throughout the process.

      I used to believe that I would be the kind of woman who, like Goldie Hawn and Kurt Russell, didn't desire marriage. However, in November, I had a moment of clarity and realized that I had allowed societal influences to taint and dilute my true desires. It became evident to me that I was meant to be a wife and that I did indeed desire marriage, despite having experienced a failed one in my youth. I decided to challenge myself by discarding all societal stereotypes. And in doing so, I discovered that marriage is my true calling. I am proud to say that I am a wife, and I am worthy of being one!

**Journal Prompt:** Checking in With Your Real Desires

Reflecting on your journey towards embracing marriage and acknowledging your true desires can be a powerful exercise. Take a moment to check in with your real desires and reflect on your evolving perspective on marriage.

- Write about your journey, considering how societal expectations may have influenced your initial beliefs. Explore the turning point when you realized that you were called to be a wife and desired marriage. How did this realization make you feel? Did it bring about any fears or uncertainties?

- Describe the process of challenging societal stereotypes and how it enabled you to discover your true calling.

Reflect on your newfound sense of worthiness as a wife.

- How has this realization shaped your outlook on relationships and the future?

Finally, consider how you can continue to honor your authentic desires and maintain a strong sense of self amidst societal pressures.

*Journal here*

**Prayer Prompt:** Checking in With Your Real Desires

Dear Heavenly Father,

 I come before You today with a heart full of gratitude for the journey You have led me on towards embracing marriage and understanding my true desires. Thank You for the opportunity to reflect on my evolving perspective on marriage and the ways societal expectations may have influenced my initial beliefs.

 As I delve into this reflection, I ask for your guidance and wisdom to help me explore the turning point when I realized that I was called to be a wife and desired marriage. Please reveal to me the emotions, fears, and uncertainties that arose during this realization. Help me to process and understand these feelings and grant me the courage to confront and overcome any obstacles in my path.

 Lord, I acknowledge that challenging societal stereotypes have played a significant role in discovering my true calling. Thank You for empowering me to question and challenge these expectations, which has enabled me to find my authentic desires and purpose. I pray that You continue to strengthen me in this process, helping me to remain steadfast in my convictions and to trust in your plan for my life.

 As I reflect on my newfound sense of worthiness as a wife, I am humbled by your grace and love. Thank You for affirming my value and worth, and for reminding me that I am deserving of a loving and fulfilling marriage. This realization has shaped my outlook on relationships and the future, allowing me to approach them with hope and a deepened understanding of your design for marriage.

 Lord, in the face of societal pressures, I ask for your guidance in honoring my authentic desires and maintaining a strong sense of self. Help me to discern your will and to stay true to my convictions, even when faced with opposition or doubt. Grant me the strength and confidence to navigate the expectations of others while remaining grounded in your truth.

 Thank You, Father, for the opportunity to reflect on my journey and desires. I surrender them all to You, trusting that You will continue to lead me on the path that aligns with your perfect plan for my life.

 In Jesus' name, I pray.

 Amen.

*My Prayer....*

# Day 11: Managing Expectations

**Scripture:** "Trust in the Lord with all your heart and lean not on your own understanding; in all your ways submit to Him, and He will make your paths straight." - Proverbs 3:5-6

God has a divine plan for each of our lives, and He knows the perfect timing for everything. If you have yet to find the right person, do not feel disheartened or think that you have missed your chance. Trust in the Lord with all your heart and do not rely solely on your own understanding. Surrender yourself to Him in all your ways, and He will bring the right person into your life at the appointed time. Remember, everything that is destined for you will always be yours and whatever is destined for you will not miss you.

Maintain unwavering faith and patience and keep your heart open to the wonderful blessings that God has in store for you. This passage of scripture holds a deep-rooted connection in my heart, as it adorned my grandmother's voicemail during my formative years. It served as a reminder to trust in the Lord, to avoid succumbing to worldly standards, and to not settle for anything less than God's best. Let us hold steadfast to our faith and values, for the world may normalize unrealistic expectations, but we can find support and guidance in the wisdom of our heavenly Father.

**Journal Prompt:** Managing Expectations

- Am I approaching potential suitors with a critical mindset?

- Are my expectations for a spouse unrealistic or overly demanding?

*Journal here*

**Prayer Prompt:** Managing Expectations

Dear God,

    I come to You today with an open heart, ready to receive your guidance and wisdom. Help me to remain faithful, trusting that You have a special plan for my life and that the right man will find me at the right time.

    Please help me to understand that passing up certain people was not because I was too picky, but because they were not meant for me. Give me the discernment to recognize red flags, trauma, and other reasons to walk away, but also help me to see when I am being too judgmental or superficial.

    I pray that You will bring someone into my life who shares my values and beliefs, and who will support me in my faith journey. Help me to trust in your timing and to submit to your will in all things.

    Thank You for your love and guidance, and for always being with me on this journey.

    Amen.

*My Prayer....*

# Day 12: Making Room: Level of Conviction.

**Scripture**: "Do not be unequally yoked with unbelievers. For what partnership has righteousness with lawlessness? Or what fellowship has light with darkness?" - 2 Corinthians 6:14

This verse encourages believers to carefully consider the relationships they form and to avoid being unequally yoked with those who do not share their faith or values. It emphasizes the importance of seeking godly connections and partnerships, including in marriage, so that the relationship can be built on a strong foundation of shared beliefs and values.

    I woke up one morning and God was telling me that the relationships I have with men, currently, aren't Godly relationships. These men are waiting for the shoe to drop so they can slide in, and that is not a healthy friendship. So, I had to go and put all of my relationships with men under a microscope. Interestingly enough, I have done that with women and have beautiful friendships. But with men, I have never done that. I was trying to hang onto them as an excuse for friendship since we had never had intimate relations.

    An example of this: I found myself entertaining an unhealed and ungodly man for months. During the course of our situationship I underwent surgery for my fibroids. Despite being fully aware of the significant day and time, this gentleman failed to reach out to me after the procedure, nor did he make any attempt to connect with me in the following days. After a heartfelt conversation with this gentleman, his response to me was that I am a strong woman who does not require his support due to the way I provide for myself. I dissected and analyzed this comment, ultimately leading to one profound realization- he is simply not the person for me.

    The signs of his lack of connection with God were present from the beginning. However, it was his failure to show up and be there for me during a crucial moment that truly highlighted his lack of regard. It was unsettling and hurtful. It was the one opportunity he had to show up and support me, and he blew it. Instead of taking accountability, he made excuses. He even went as far as having his father, a pastor, facetime me and express that his wife had to teach him how to show up as a husband for her. I comprehended the message while also being aware that his life is out of order. Teaching a man when to be supportive of you is one thing; attempting to alter his ingrained response is quite another. God states, a man should love his wife like he loves the church. Once I knew his love for God wasn't a priority, I should have opted out, understanding he didn't have the capacity to love and value me as God says. I had to respectfully tell Pastor that his wife taught him that in his 20's and I'm sure the learning curve wasn't as critical as undergoing surgery and being put under general anesthesia. Pastor agreed! God made me so uncomfortable with everything that came out of his son's mouth. I heard His voice in my body, this gave me chills and I was convicted! Now, my level of conviction led me to not disregard this as a mere coincidence, but to recognize it as a dealbreaker. It became clear to me that I cannot allow such behavior in a relationship.

    In life, it is crucial for us to pay attention to the signs that are presented to us. We must never ignore those instances where someone's actions don't align with what we deserve and desire in a relationship. It is through self-reflection and understanding that we come to the realization that certain individuals are not meant to be a part of our journey. And so, we must have the strength and courage to let go, to release what no longer serves us, and to trust that the right person, the one who will show up and show out for us, will come into our lives at the perfect time.

Remember, that you deserve someone who not only cherishes and respects you, but also understands the importance of accountability and presence. Trust in the process and have faith that God has someone extraordinary in store for you. Keep shining your light and never settle for anything less than what you truly deserve.

**Journal prompt**: Making Room: Level of Conviction.

Reflect on your relationships with men and consider if they align with God's plan for your life. Take a moment to put these relationships under a microscope and evaluate if they are truly godly friendships.

- o Are there any signs that these relationships may not be healthy or aligned with your values? How have these relationships affected your journey towards finding a godly spouse?
- o In what ways can you create space in your life for a future husband?

Explore your thoughts and feelings about this process of examination and discernment and consider how you can actively seek a godly relationship that aligns with your faith and values.

*Journal here*

**Prayer Prompt:** Making Room: Level of Conviction.

Dear God,

Grant me the wisdom to discern the nature of my relationships. Help me to identify those that align with your word and your plan for my life. Give me the courage to let go of relationships that do not glorify You or promote a Godly lifestyle. As I journey towards finding a spouse, guide me in creating healthy, meaningful connections that reflect your love and grace. Teach me to make space in my life for my future husband and prepare my heart to receive him. Above all, may my life and relationships always honor You.

>In Jesus' name, I pray,

>Amen.

*My Prayer....*

# Day 13: Nourishing Your Soul

**Scripture:** "Above all else, guard your heart, for everything you do flows from it. - Proverbs 4:23

"Do not be misled: 'Bad company corrupts good character.'"1 Corinthians 15:33

    Nourishing your soul is pivotal. You must spend time with God daily, starting as soon as you rise, through devotion, prayer, meditation, and music. Take moments throughout the day for clarity. I find that my best prayers are in my car, before I go into the house.
    While it may be challenging for some to accept, nourishing your soul with righteousness is essential. It involves being mindful of the content you listen to, watch, and engage with. I can relate to this personally, as I used to listen to R&B music during moments of sorrow. However, I soon discovered that it only deepened my sadness. By choosing uplifting and positive content, you actively guard your heart and mind, ensuring that you nourish your soul with devotion and righteousness. It may require effort and conscious decision-making, but the rewards are truly worth it. Mindless scrolling takes hours of our day, so surround yourself with content that aligns with your faith and values, and you will find reassurance, strength, and lasting joy.
    The transfer of energy and spirit is a genuine phenomenon. This applies not only to the content we consume but also to the food we eat. Certain foods can increase blood sugar, plaque in arteries, and blood pressure, which can lead to health issues such as hypertension, diabetes, and high cholesterol. It's important to be mindful of what we eat to ensure our overall well-being. When you eat, choose something healthy. Now, I'm not saying that I'm perfect or that I never indulge in fatty foods like ice cream

or donuts, but I strive to cook healthy meals five days out of seven. I have found that daily fasting contributes to a sharper mind and clarity.

Let us embrace a biblical perspective that uplifts and reassures. Fill yourself with the word, healthy food, and positivity, for they will bring comfort and strength. Choose content that aligns with your faith and values, as it will empower and inspire you. By doing so, you actively invite divine blessings into your life. Trust in the power of God's word to transform your mindset and bring everlasting joy.

Remember, you have the power to shape your environment and nourish your soul. Surround yourself with uplifting content, choose healthy food, and spend time with God. In doing so, you will find inspiration, motivation, and the strength to overcome any challenges that come your way. Keep your heart and mind focused on righteousness and watch as divine blessings unfold in your life.

**Journal Prompt:** Nourishing Your Soul

- How does the content I consume such as: music, movies, or books affect my mood and emotions? Have I noticed any patterns of negative energy or sadness when engaging with certain types of content?

- How can I be more mindful and selective in choosing content that aligns with my faith and values?

- How can I incorporate healthy choices into my daily routine and make it a habit that aligns with my faith and values whilst actively inviting godliness and positivity into my mind and heart?

- How do I believe this intentional nourishment of my soul can bring peace, strength, and divine blessings into my life?

- How can I trust in the power of God's word to transform my mindset?

Reflect on these questions and write down your thoughts and intentions. Use this opportunity to deepen your understanding of how taking care of your physical health through healthy eating and conscious content consumption aligns with your faith and values and how it can contribute to the nourishment of your soul. By nourishing both your soul and your body, you are showing God that you value and appreciate the gift of life and are taking care of yourself from the inside out. This holistic approach to well-being can lead to a greater sense of overall fulfillment and a deeper connection to your faith.

*Journal here*

**Prayer Prompt:** Nourishing Your Soul

Dear God,

  Thank you, Lord, for the gift of nourishing food and the ability to make choices that honor my body, which You have blessed me with. I recognize that taking care of my physical health is not only an act of self-care, but also a way to show gratitude to You for providing me with sustenance. Help me to view healthy eating as an opportunity to appreciate and take care of the body You have given me.
  Lord, I acknowledge that by prioritizing both the nourishment of my soul and my body, I am demonstrating my commitment to living a holistically healthy life. I understand that taking care of my physical health contributes to my ability to nourish my soul and live a righteous life. Grant me the strength and discipline to incorporate healthy food choices into my daily routine and make it a habit that aligns with my faith and values.
  I am grateful for the opportunity to have options when it comes to the food I consume. As long as I have breath, I have options (Hoodhealer, 2019). I thank You for the wisdom and discernment to make healthy choices that will benefit my well-being. Help me to show appreciation for your provisions by making conscious decisions to nourish my body with good food and content.

  In Jesus' name, I pray.

  Amen.

  Take a moment to pray this prayer expressing your gratitude for the gift of healthy food and the ability to make choices that honor your body and soul. Use this prayer as a reminder to approach your food choices with mindfulness and gratitude, recognizing that they are a reflection of your faith and desire to take care of yourself from within.

*My Prayer....*

# Day 14: Showing Gratitude

**Scripture:** "Give thanks in all circumstances; for this is the will of God in Christ Jesus for you." - 1 Thessalonians 5:18

I express my gratitude to God every day by starting my day with worship and prayer. Putting Him first is always my priority. I believe in showing random acts of kindness and striving to be inoffensive, spreading positivity, and embodying the values that God teaches. I also give back to my community by exchanging my services for fresh fruit from a farm, workout sessions for therapy, and contributing to God through tithing and offerings, even when I am not able to attend church. Even when I face trials and tribulations, I choose to praise because I believe that these difficult times are temporary and better things are likely to come soon.

Showing God gratitude is a crucial aspect of maintaining healthy relationships, including marriage. When we express gratitude, we are acknowledging and appreciating the efforts of God and our spouse, which can deepen our connection and strengthen our bond. It also fosters a culture of positivity and mutual respect, which can help us navigate difficult times together.

Furthermore, gratitude helps us cultivate a more optimistic mindset, which can make us more resilient when facing adversity. This can be especially helpful in marriage, where there will be the inevitable ebbs and flows. When we approach our relationships with a grateful heart, we are more likely to focus on the positive aspects of our marriage, even during difficult times.

Ultimately, showing gratitude can help us build a strong foundation of love, respect, and appreciation, which are essential qualities for any successful marriage led by God! Be a mirror!

**Journal Prompt:** Showing Gratitude

Reflect on a time when you felt grateful for something or someone in your life.

- What were the circumstances? How did you express your gratitude? What impact did it have on your relationship with that person or your overall attitude towards life?

*Journal here*

**Prayer Prompt:** Showing Gratitude

Gracious God,

In this moment of prayer, I want to express my profound gratitude for the future husband You have planned for me. I have faith that You are guiding our paths to cross at the perfect time, and I eagerly await the day when we will join our lives together. I trust in your divine plan and timing, knowing that You will bring us together when the time is right.

Thank you, dear God, for granting me a husband who will be my rock, my confidant, and my best friend. I have faith that he will possess the qualities I hope to find in a partner - integrity, kindness, and compassion. I am grateful for his love, loyalty, and unwavering commitment to our marriage.

I express my gratitude for the ways in which You will bless our union and guide us on this journey together. I have faith that You will nurture and cherish our relationship, helping us grow closer to each other and to You. I am grateful for the love and support we will share, and for the strength we will draw from our faith in You.

I pray that I may always be a source of gratitude and love for my future husband. May I show him appreciation for his presence in my life, celebrating the big and small moments together. Help me to be a supportive wife, a loving companion, and a source of strength for him, just as he will be for me.

Guide me, O Lord, to continually honor and appreciate my future husband. May my words and actions reflect the faith I hold in my heart for him. And as we journey through life together, may our love and bond grow stronger with each passing day.

Thank you, dear God, for the privilege of praying for my future husband. I have faith in your divine plan and timing, and I know that You will bring us together when the time is right. Until then, I will continue to express my gratitude and prepare my heart for the love that awaits.

    In your loving and guiding presence, I offer this prayer.

    Amen.

*My Prayer....*

# Day 15: Are You Who You Want to Marry?

**Scripture:** "As water reflects the face, so one's life reflects the heart." -Proverbs 27:19

This scripture reminds us that our outward actions and behaviors are a reflection of what lies within our hearts. When we prioritize our spiritual growth, self-care, and commitment to God it radiates through our actions and influences those around us. By embodying the qualities, we seek in a partner, we create an environment that attracts individuals who share our values and desire a deep connection with God.

It is important to lead by example when attracting a future husband who shares your godly values and standards of personal care. I know many people who are requesting God to send them a perfect husband. I've heard things such as, "I won't talk to a man with braces", "My man must be over the height of 6' 2 ", or "He must have a luxury vehicle." Meanwhile, they haven't discussed his relationship with God, the quality of his prayers, or where he is at in his walk with Christ. Stating this, I ask you to hold yourself to the same standards you require. The fact is we're all imperfect.

In the same breath, you should be doing regular upkeep on yourself. Embracing personal hygiene practices, such as regular showers, dental care, and a commitment to overall well-being, reflects a reverence for the body that God has blessed us with. By taking care of ourselves physically, we honor the temple that houses our spirit.

When seeking a partner, remember that compatibility extends beyond superficial traits. Instead, focus on finding someone who shares your deep connection with God, self-love, and personal growth. By embodying the qualities, you desire in a spouse, you will attract a like-minded individual who appreciates and respects your commitment to living a godly and wholesome life.

As you strive to be the person you wish to attract, remember that true love is built on a foundation of shared values, mutual respect, and a desire to support each other's spiritual journey. Embrace your own spirituality and personal care, and trust that by doing so, you will attract a partner who aligns with your aspirations and shares your commitment to a godly and fulfilling relationship.

**Journal Prompt:** Are You Who You Want to Marry?

Reflect on your own personal care practices and spiritual growth.

- o How can you further prioritize these aspects of your life and lead by example in attracting a husband who shares your Godly values?

*Journal here*

**Prayer Prompt:** Are You Who You Want to Marry?

Dear Lord,

  Thank You for the gift of marriage and the opportunity to find a future who shares my godly values. I understand that seeking a spouse goes beyond finding someone to have a relationship with, but rather someone to enter into a lifelong commitment of love and support.

  As I strive to lead by example in my personal care practices and spiritual growth, I pray that You guide me towards a husband who also prioritizes these aspects of their life. Help me to embody the qualities I desire in a spouse, so that I may attract someone who shares my commitment to living a godly and fulfilling marriage.

  I pray that my actions and choices reflect the love and devotion I have for You, Lord. May I be a living testament of your grace and goodness, and may that radiate through me to attract a husband who is equally dedicated to their relationship with You.

  In this journey of seeking a godly spouse, I ask for your guidance and discernment. Help me to recognize and discern the person who aligns with my values, who will walk beside me in this lifelong commitment of marriage. May our union be a reflection of your love and bring glory to your name.

  I trust in your divine timing and plan, Lord. As I continue to prioritize my personal care and spiritual growth, I pray that You prepare both my heart and the heart of my future spouse for the beautiful and sacred union of marriage.

  In your name, I pray.

  Amen.

*My Prayer....*

# Day 16: How Do I Want to Feel in My Marriage?

**Scripture**: "Love is patient, love is kind. It does not envy, it does not boast, it is not proud. It does not dishonor others, it is not self-seeking, it is not easily angered, it keeps no record of wrongs. Love does not delight in evil but rejoices with the truth. It always protects, always trusts, always hopes, always perseveres." - 1 Corinthians 13:4-7

I remember past relationships where I paid no heed to the signs - the feeling of walking on eggshells or being overly expressive. I remember a date where my pulse altered and I thought to myself, this isn't normal. Yet, I'd still continue with this person, even when my body was clearly expressing discomfort, despite no words being spoken. Often, we turn a blind eye to the signals our bodies send us.

Take a friend of mine and his relationship, for instance. He developed psoriasis and skin discoloration due to the stress he was experiencing in his relationship. He knew deep down that the person he was with wasn't right for him, but he forced himself to continue. His skin broke out as a physical manifestation of his internal struggle.

In the intricate dance of relationships, oftentimes we overlook the subtle whispers of unease, the whispers of disquiet, and the whispers of anxiety. In our pursuit of love, we unintentionally disregard the signs that indicate our souls are not at ease. Unbeknownst to us, we remain in this state, oblivious to the fact that our Creator is not a harbinger of confusion.

My message to you is this: Listen to your body. Pay attention to that voice in your head or the way your heart might skip a beat. Be so attuned with yourself that you can recognize the shift - whether good or bad - when someone is in your presence.

Remember, your body communicates with you in subtle ways. Listen to it. Trust it. It's usually God speaking to you and through you.

When embarking upon the sacred path to matrimony, let us pause and reflect upon the essence of our being. Consider the profound impact this union will have upon our very existence. Contemplate how you yearn to feel in the presence of your chosen companion. Ponder the harmonious rhythm of your heart, the gentle cadence that reverberates when your souls intertwine. Reflect upon the serenity that envelops you, cradling you in its tender embrace as you slumber. Meditate upon the profound reactions that stir within you, the emotions that surge forth, and the visceral response that resonates to their touch.

For, verily, I have witnessed countless souls traversing the vast tapestry of life, entering into unions yet finding afflictions that manifest upon their very flesh. These ailments, not borne of carnal desires but rather the burdensome weight of stress, manifest in the form of psoriasis, lost edges, weight gain or loss, or yeast infections. Thus, let us be mindful and attentive. Let us attune ourselves to the way in which our chosen companion makes us feel. Let us discern the gentle whispers of our spirit as it dances in response to their presence.

In this pursuit of love, may our souls find happiness, our spirits find harmony, and our beings find profound fulfillment. May we heed the signs, for they are the guideposts that lead us towards a union bathed in tranquility, serenity, and everlasting love. Remember that marriage isn't always happy, but it should ALWAYS be HOLY!

**Journal Prompt:** How Do I Want to Feel in My Marriage?

Reflect upon a past relationship where you may have ignored the signs of unease or discomfort.

- o   Write about the physical or emotional manifestations that occurred and how they affected you. Consider how you can learn from this experience and apply it to future relationships.

Explore ways in which you can become more attuned to your body's signals and listen to your intuition.

- o   How can you prioritize your own well-being and ensure that you are in a healthy and fulfilling relationship?

*Journal here*

**Prayer prompt:** How Do I Want to Feel in My Marriage?

God,

In this sacred moment, I humbly come before You, seeking your guidance and grace. As I embark on the journey towards marriage, I beseech You to bless my union with profound understanding and unwavering love.

Grant me the wisdom to recognize the signs that speak to the depths of my soul, those whispers of unease, disease, and anxiety. Help me discern the true nature of my emotions, to unravel the mysteries that lie within my heart.

In your infinite wisdom, You have reminded me that You are not a God of confusion. As I intertwine my life and spirit with my assigned husband, I ask for clarity and discernment. Allow me to recognize how I truly desire to feel when I am with him, the melodies that resonate within my heart, and the peace that envelops me as I slumber.

Grant me the ability to attune myself to the subtle nuances of my being, to listen to the whispers of my spirit and the echoes of my soul. Help me pay attention to the way in which my God appointed husband makes me feel, to the responses that stir within me and the reactions that manifest upon my very being.

God, I humbly ask for guidance and protection as I navigate the sacred path to marriage. May my union be blessed with profound love, understanding, and fulfillment. May my soul find warmth in my husband's presence and my spirit dance in harmonious rhythm.

In your divine grace, I find strength and reassurance. I surrender my heart and spirit to your wisdom, trusting in your guiding hand. May my marriage be a testament to your love and grace, a beacon of light and inspiration to all who witness it.

With gratitude in my heart, I offer this prayer, knowing that You hear my humble plea.

In Jesus heavenly name.

Amen.

## *My Prayer....*

# Day 17: My Ultimate Dream

**Scripture:** "Delight yourself in the Lord, and He will give you the desires of your heart." - Psalm 37:4

This verse encourages us to focus on our relationship with God and trust that He will provide what we need and desire, including a partner. It also reminds us to be patient and wait on God's timing, knowing that He has a plan for our lives.

My ultimate dream is to establish a profound and meaningful relationship with God and for Him to use all my talents while I'm here. I aspire to pray for and help future generations shed the weight of fear and anxiety that often plagues society. My aim is to remove the societal barriers that prevent people from nurturing their relationship with God and sharing it with others. By doing so, people can live their lives to the fullest, free from the constraints of society or work unburdened by pride and offense and allowing them to trust themselves.

I pray to grow old in a healthy and loving marriage with a partner who shares my beliefs and values, and who also dreams of creating a life together. Our union should not only bring us joy but also serve as a source of inspiration and positivity for those around us. By nurturing a deep connection with God and sharing our love and wisdom with others, we can leave a lasting legacy of love and impact that will endure for generations to come. I pray that my God given partner and I live healthy and prosperous lives by being servants of God through our travels and creating generational wealth with our talents.

**Journal Prompt:** My Ultimate Dream

- What is your ultimate dream in life and partnership? How do you see yourself and your partner achieving this dream?

- What role does faith play in making your dreams a reality?

*Journal here*

**Prayer Prompt:** My Ultimate Dream

Heavenly Father,

    I come before You today with a grateful heart, thanking You for the plans You have for my life. I thank You for the dreams and aspirations that You have placed in my heart, and for the partner that You will give me to journey with. Lord, I pray that You guide me as I seek to fulfill Your plan for my life and prepare me for the partner You have in store for me. Help me to trust in You and to lean on You for guidance and direction. I pray that You give me the strength and wisdom to overcome any obstacles that may stand in the way of my dreams. May my future marriage be a reflection of your love and grace, and may I always seek to honor You in all that I do.

    In Jesus' name, I pray.

    Amen.

*My Prayer....*

*Part Two: Building the Wife*

*"Building requires a certain level of couth. You must become her daily through practice and prayer."*
*~ Dr. Dawn*

# Day 18: Limited Access

**Scripture:** "Or do you not know that your body is a temple of the Holy Spirit within you, whom you have from God? You are not your own, for you were bought with a price. So, glorify God in your body." - 1 Corinthians 6:19-20

This verse reminds us of the importance of honoring and respecting our bodies and treating them as sacred vessels for the Holy Spirit. It encourages us to make choices that align with our faith and to prioritize our well-being in all aspects of life, including relationships.

The current climate supports women being in their Lori Harvey era. This is not a criticism of Lori, but rather an observation. People often desire love, but they may not consider the necessary steps to achieve a safe and healthy marriage. It is important to prioritize protecting your body beyond just exchanging energy. You can't be with anyone and everyone. Being with multiple partners can potentially impact your ability to conceive in the future, and I encourage you to do your own research on this topic. The emotional trauma to your soul is priceless.

Allowing people to have access to you and limiting your thoughts to the bare minimum promotes a scarcity mindset. Those who have a scarcity mindset often experience limitations in their relationships and lives because they don't believe in limitless possibilities. However, it's important to understand that this mindset requires a relationship with God, as well as healing and self-confidence.

Just like the food you consume, everything you put in or on your body can have an impact. If women fully understood their ability to shape the male/female climate, there would be more successful marriages. I challenge you to not give everyone access to your mental, physical, or emotional space, as doing so can cloud your judgment. Remember that you attract people who are on a similar emotional level as you and frequent where you frequent.

I always tell my friends that it's interesting because I, as a single woman with a strong faith, tend to attract godly men. They see my positive energy. I know that I won't meet my future husband at a bar or similar places. It's essential to ensure that the people you surround yourself with and the places you frequent align with your goals. That doesn't mean you have to be boring. I still go out with girlfriends, enjoy concerts and comedy clubs, but I'm mindful that my outfits and choices reflect the kind of person I am and the type of husband I want to attract.

So, keep in mind that the people you attract, such as cheaters, men who seek attention on social media, or those who fly women out, may be a reflection or projection of where you are on your personal journey. I'm not suggesting you become a nun, as there is nothing wrong with that either. However, there is a certain posture required to receive the blessings that God has in store for you. This posture is built on prayer, positioning yourself correctly, and exercising discipline and delayed gratification.

Don't allow men access to you who disrupt your peace, have "potential", taint your mind, or enjoy your body while you're preparing for your future husband. I'm not playing house! I did that when I was a child with my Barbies, and even then, they were married in my dollhouse.

**Journal Prompt:** Limited Access

- What energy do you want to project out into the world for your future husband to find you? And how are you going to change the amount of access you allow men and people, in general, to have to you?

- What are some areas in your life where you have a scarcity mindset?

*Journal here*

**Prayer Prompt:** Limited Access

Father God,

    I come before You today with a humble heart, seeking guidance and strength in my journey for a godly husband to find me. I thank You for the reminder that my body is a temple of the Holy Spirit and I am not my own. Help me to honor and respect this sacred vessel in all aspects of my life.

    Father, I pray that You align my energy with your will, so that I may project the qualities and values that will attract the man You have prepared for me. Grant me the wisdom to make choices that align with my faith and to prioritize my well-being. Help me to understand the importance of protecting my body and emotional well-being from those who may not have sincere intentions.

    Lord, I ask for your guidance in changing the amount of access I allow men and people to have to me. Help me to set healthy boundaries that protect my mental, physical, and emotional space. Give me discernment to recognize those who may disrupt my peace or taint my mind. Give me the strength to keep them at a distance.

    Father, I pray for a posture of readiness to receive the blessings You have in store for me. Teach me to position myself correctly, to exercise discipline, and have delayed gratification. Help me to cultivate a mindset of abundance, knowing that You have limitless possibilities for my life.

    Lord, I surrender my scarcity mindset to You. Heal any areas of my life where I doubt your provision and limit my own potential. Fill me with your love and confidence, knowing that I am deserving of a healthy and fulfilling marriage.

Thank You, Lord, for hearing my prayer. I trust in your perfect timing and plan for my life. May I continue to seek You in all things and glorify You in my body.

In Jesus' name, I pray.

Amen.

*My Prayer....*

# Day 19: While Single

**Scripture:** "Now to the unmarried and the widows I say: It is good for them to stay unmarried, as I do." - 1 Corinthians 7:8

This scripture highlights the apostle Paul's perspective on singleness. He acknowledges that it can be beneficial for some individuals to remain unmarried, just as he himself chose to be. It suggests that being single can be a valid and meaningful way of living, allowing individuals to focus on their relationship with God and serve Him wholeheartedly.

The topic of being single is interesting because many people equate it with being lonely, which is not the proper equation. While you're single, it's the opportune time to learn about yourself, spend time with yourself, strengthen your relationship with God, serve, travel, and build both money and generational wealth. It's about personal growth. During my own single period, I achieved three out of my five degrees and my relationship with God was strengthened because I needed Him. When I got divorced, I only had $3.73 to my name and a full tank of gas, so it was nothing but the grace of God that got me through those moments.

Being single is also a time to teach yourself how to deal with your inner thoughts and distinguish the voice in your head from yourself, God, and even the devil or what people call the "bad angel" on your other shoulder. It was during my single period that I began looking for a home church. I heightened my level of atonement and my prayer life. I determined what type of friends and people I wanted in my life. It was during this time that I learned not to function in hustle mode because the frequency of that is very low. Instead, I focused on functioning and flourishing, which is a completely different vibration that I radiated into the world.

I saved up money and time-off. I got my first passport as a single woman. I've always craved to learn about different cultures and even study other people's religions because how can you teach people about something without knowing about it yourself? Through travel, I learned how to problem solve and travel solo. Many people would say it's unsafe for a woman to travel alone, but I did it anyway. I took off work for 30 days because I had so much paid time off (PTO) that could be cashed out or accrued. I apologize, this was 10 years ago, and I know PTO policies have changed since then- probably because of me. Sorry y'all! I even started traveling with my kids and got them passports. They have TSA and global entry. They even get to go to the lounge at the airport. I created an atmosphere of growth and showed them the experiences life has to offer.

I became an avid book reader and increased my home library. It's funny because my children now love to read too. I got hobbies. Most importantly, during this period, I found myself. Singleness is a time to find yourself, as the popular buzzword says, wholeness! I became the most intentional mother I could be, ensuring that my children got the best of me, not the stressed-out and tired pieces. They know that I'm capable of feeling that way, but they also see that I turn to God. Whenever they experience anything, they ask me, "Mom, can we pray?" and I love that. I taught them that your past doesn't have to dictate your future; instead, it's your prayer life, your relationship with God, your willingness to serve, and being present that shape your future.

As mentioned, some individuals are meant to be single and serve. Everyone has a unique path in life, and for some, being single allows them to dedicate their time and energy to serving others and fulfilling their purpose in different ways. It's important to listen to God's calling and follow the path that aligns with our values and desires.

Remember, being single is not a limitation, but an opportunity for personal growth, self-discovery, and making a positive impact in the world. Embrace this phase of your life. Continue to nurture your relationship with God and be open to the possibilities that lie ahead.

**Journal Prompt:** While Single

- How has being single or going through a period of personal growth impacted your relationship with God?

- In what ways have you used this time to strengthen your prayer life and seek guidance from God?

- What activities or hobbies have you pursued during this time that have brought you joy and helped you discover more about yourself?

- Have you encountered any challenges or moments of loneliness during this period? How did you turn to God for comfort and guidance?

*Journal here*

**Prayer Prompt:** While Single

Dear Heavenly Father,

    Thank You for the gift of singleness and the opportunities it presents for personal growth and self-discovery. I am grateful for the wisdom shared in 1 Corinthians 7:8, which has reminded us that being single can be a meaningful way of living.

    During my journey of singleness, I have witnessed your presence and guidance in my life. Through prayer, I have sought your wisdom and discernment, which allows me to navigate my thoughts and distinguish between different voices. You have helped me to quiet the noise and hear your voice clearly, guiding me towards the path that aligns with your will.

    There have been moments of uncertainty and loneliness, but in those moments, I turned to You for comfort and guidance. Your love and grace have provided me with strength and assurance that I am not alone. You have shown me that my relationship with You is the most important, and through that, I have found peace and contentment.

    Through prayer, I have also found clarity in my decision-making. You have given me the courage to make choices that align with my values and desires, even if they may be different from societal expectations. My faith has shaped my perspective on singleness, allowing me to see it as an opportunity for personal growth, self-discovery, and serving others.

    In my single season, I have seen how my prayer life has influenced my relationships. I have learned the importance of surrounding myself with positive and supportive individuals who uplift and encourage my faith journey. Through prayer, I have sought guidance in building healthy and meaningful connections with others, and You have blessed me with a community that supports and understands my journey.

Thank You, Lord, for the lessons learned and the growth experienced during my single season. I pray that You continue to strengthen my relationship with You, guide my thoughts and decisions, and use me to make a positive impact in the world. Help me to embrace this phase of my life fully and to trust in your perfect timing for all things.

In Jesus' name, I pray.

Amen.

*My Prayer....*

# Day 20: The Storms Within

**Scripture:** "Submit yourselves, then, to God. Resist the devil, and he will flee from you. Come near to God and He will come near to you. Wash your hands, you sinners, and purify your hearts, you double-minded." - James 4:7-8

  This scripture encourages us to submit ourselves to God and resist the devil's temptations. It reminds us that when we draw near to God, He will draw near to us, providing us with the strength and guidance to overcome our temptations. It emphasizes the importance of purifying our hearts and staying focused on our commitment to God, which can be achieved through prayer and seeking His presence in our lives.

  "The Storm" is a portion of the book where I have to be so raw. I'm risking judgment, but I don't care. When thinking about this journey, I don't want to make it sound like I'm superhuman and that I don't have worldly desires and temptations. I prayed my way through the storm, and for the most part, I can truly say it's easy. But when it's not, and I hear that not-so-good voice in my head- I know it's prayer time.

  I will let your level of conviction guide you on where to go and how to stand, firm and honest with yourself and God. For me, my storms are craving touch, companionship, entertaining the void by hopping on the phone, and masturbation due to celibacy. Let me educate on how to combat these temptations. When it comes to masturbation, I have cut out pornography, which is something that I used to watch. In my head, I justified it by saying, "Well, I'm not having sex," but then I realized I was causing myself to get into another unrealistic addiction that controlled my mind. So, I removed pornography altogether, which took prayer and self-control. I don't put anything inside my vagina at all because when my husband comes, I want him to fill that gap and know that I waited for him against all societal temptations. I waited. I don't crave touch often, but when I do, I fill that void with my body pillow. Thankfully, I also have children, so I can cuddle with them to fulfill this desire. Many times, I just want to hop on the phone to engage in conversation with a man. During those moments, I will find a girl friend to talk with because, as I mentioned, I got rid of male friends. And I pray.

So, the key is combating these temptations through prayer, prayer, and more prayer. I will not pretend that I have all the answers in this area. I can only tell you that my level of conviction guides me deeper into this journey, and when my husband finds me, it will be glorious. It's hard, but nothing that I've ever wanted has been easy, and that's what gets me through.

**Journal Prompt:** The Storms Within

- What temptations do I struggle with in my own life? How do they affect my relationship with God and my overall well-being?

- How can I actively resist these temptations and draw closer to God? What strategies or practices can I implement to strengthen my faith and overcome these challenges?

- In what ways can I seek support from others in my journey of resisting temptations? Who can I turn to for accountability, encouragement, and prayer?

*Journal here*

**Prayer Prompt:** The Storms Within

Heavenly Father,

  I come before You today with a humble heart, acknowledging the temptations that I struggle with in my own life. You know the challenges I face and the ways in which these temptations affect my relationship with You and my overall well-being. I ask for your guidance and strength to resist these temptations and draw closer to you.

  Lord, help me to actively resist these temptations. Give me the wisdom to recognize when they arise and the courage to say no. Teach me to rely on your word and your promises, finding solace and strength in your presence. Help me to fill my mind and heart with thoughts that honor You, and to engage in practices that align with your will for my life.

  Father, I ask for your grace and forgiveness when I stumble and fall. Help me to remember that You are a loving and forgiving God, always ready to welcome me back into your arms. Give me the perseverance to continue on this journey, even when it feels difficult or overwhelming.

  Lord, I also ask for your guidance in seeking support from others. Show me who I can turn to for accountability, encouragement, and prayer. Surround me with people who will uplift and support me in my journey of resisting temptations. Help me to be open and vulnerable with those I trust, allowing them to walk alongside me and offer their support.

  I trust that the blessings and fulfillment that come from this choice will far surpass any temporary gratification. May my decision to wait bring glory to your name and ultimately lead me to a marriage that is built on a solid foundation of love, commitment, and faith.

Lord, as I resist temptations and choose to wait for my future husband, I know that I am cultivating a foundation of purity and faithfulness. By abstaining from the physical and emotional intimacy outside of marriage, I am preserving something sacred and precious for the one You have prepared for me. I am choosing to honor and respect my future husband, even before I know who he is.

In all things, Lord, I desire to draw nearer to You. Strengthen my faith, deepen my commitment to You, and help me to overcome these challenges. I know that with your help, I can resist temptation and live a life that brings honor and glory to your name.

I pray all these things in the name of Jesus,

Amen.

*My Prayer....*

# Day 21: Divorcees

**Scripture:** "But if the unbeliever leaves, let it be so. The brother or the sister is not bound in such circumstances; God has called us to live in peace." - 1 Corinthians 7:15

This verse is often understood as permitting divorce in cases where an unbelieving spouse chooses to leave the marriage. However, it's important to recognize that this passage is specifically addressing marriages between believers and non-believers and the challenges that arise in such situations.

If you've never been married, please continue reading as there are gems in this portion. The term "divorcee" can unfortunately carry a negative connotation in society, and it is disheartening to experience judgment and discrimination because of it. It's like having a metaphorical "D" on your chest, which can be quite unfair and hurtful, especially when it comes from people who have never been married or those within the church community.

It is important to remember that you are not defined by your marital status or past experiences. You should not let others shame or define you based on being divorced. Everyone's journey is unique. It is not for anyone else to judge or question the choices we have made in our lives.

I faced difficult circumstances in my previous marriage. Marrying someone significantly older, controlling, and prone to hoarding was incredibly challenging. I sought help through therapy and relied on my faith to find healing and understanding. We were not equally yoked and that doesn't warrant a lifelong, sacrificial sentence.

God wants us to be happy and holy. I'm not advocating for divorce, but rather acknowledging that sometimes it is necessary to prioritize our own physical and emotional safety and leave unhealthy relationships. My decision to end that marriage was a courageous step towards finding happiness and a healthier environment for myself and my children.

I want to encourage you to reframe how you identify yourself. You are not just a divorced person, but a strong and resilient individual who desires a loving and fulfilling marriage. Do not let others diminish your worth or try to convince you otherwise. Focus on your own growth, happiness, and desires for a future relationship.

Surround yourself with supportive and understanding people who uplift you rather than bring you down. Remember that your experiences have shaped you into the person you are today. You deserve love, happiness, and a chance at a fulfilling relationship. Trust in yourself and your journey. Don't let anyone put a big "D" on your chest! You define who you are and what you deserve. God does not want you to be in an unsafe situation or with someone who is a non-believer or even manipulates the Bible.

**Journal Prompt:** Divorcees

Reflect on how society's perception of divorce has influenced your own self-perception.

- How have you internalized any negative connotations associated with being divorced? How has this affected your self-esteem and beliefs about your worthiness of love and happiness?

Consider the strengths and resilience that you have demonstrated throughout your divorce journey.

- Write about moments where you have shown courage, determination, and growth. If you've never been divorced, write how you will take preventative measures to prevent divorce in your future marriage.
    - **Important note**- Also, remember God isn't going to send you a man that is married and isn't divorced. He is still married. God isn't a God of confusion.

*Journal here*

**Prayer Prompt:** Divorcees

Dear God,

    I come before You today with a heavy heart, burdened by the negative perceptions and judgments that society places upon those who have experienced divorce. It is disheartening to be labeled, to feel like I carry a metaphorical "D" on my chest, and to face discrimination from those who may not understand the complexities of my journey.

    But Lord, I know that my worth and identity are not defined by societal opinions or past experiences. You see me as a beloved child, created in your image, who's deserving of love, happiness, and a fulfilling relationship. Help me to internalize this truth and to let go of any negative connotations that have affected my self-esteem and beliefs about my worthiness.

    Remind me, dear Father, of the strength and resilience I have demonstrated throughout my divorce journey. In moments of struggle and pain, I found the courage to seek help, to rely on my faith, and to prioritize my safety, well-being, and that of my loved ones. These experiences have shaped me into a stronger and wiser person. I am grateful for the growth they have brought.

    Lord, I ask for your guidance and support as I navigate this journey of healing and self-discovery. Surround me with understanding and supportive people who uplift and encourage me. Help me to find solace in your love and to trust in your plan for my life.

    Grant me the wisdom to discern healthy relationships and the strength to let go of those that do not align with your will. Fill my heart with hope and excitement for the future, knowing that You desire my happiness and holiness.

In your infinite grace, heal any wounds that have been caused by the judgments and discrimination I have faced. Renew my self-esteem and restore my belief in my worthiness of love, happiness, and a fulfilling relationship.

Thank You, Lord, for your unwavering love and for the opportunity to grow and thrive despite life's challenges. May I always remember that I am defined by your love and grace, not by my past experiences.

In Jesus' name, I pray.

Amen.

*My Prayer....*

# Day 22: Being the Virtuous Woman I am Assigned to Be

**Scripture:**

10 An excellent wife who can find?
   She is far more precious than rubies.
11 The heart of her husband trusts in her,
   and he will have no lack of gain.
12 She does him good, and not harm,
   all the days of her life.
13 She seeks wool and flax,
   and works with willing hands.
14 She is like the ships of the merchant;
   she brings her food from afar.
15 She rises while it is yet night
   and provides food for her household
   and portions for her maidens.
16 She considers a field and buys it;
   with the fruit of her hands she plants a vineyard.
17 She dresses herself with strength
   and makes her arms strong.
18 She perceives that her merchandise is profitable.
   Her lamp does not go out at night.
19 She puts her hands to the distaff,
   and her hands hold the spindle.
20 She opens her hand to the poor
   and reaches out her hands to the needy.
21 She is not afraid of snow for her household,
   for all her household are clothed in scarlet.
22 She makes bed coverings for herself;
   her clothing is fine linen and purple.
23 Her husband is known in the gates
   when he sits among the elders of the land.

24 She makes linen garments and sells them;
   she delivers sashes to the merchant.
25 Strength and dignity are her clothing,
   and she laughs at the time to come.
26 She opens her mouth with wisdom,   and the teaching of kindness is on her tongue.
27 She looks well to the ways of her household
   and does not eat the bread of idleness.
28 Her children rise up and call her blessed;
   her husband also, and he praises her:
29 "Many women have done excellently,
   but you surpass them all."
30 Charm is deceitful, and beauty is vain,
   but a woman who fears the Lord is to be praised.
31 Give her of the fruit of her hands,
   and let her works praise her in the gates.

   - Proverbs 31:10-31

     I embrace my role as a helpmate; constantly striving to be a beacon of creativity, intelligence, and unwavering kindness. I am also a loyal friend; always there to support and uplift those around me. Beyond that, I am also a devoted mother; dedicating my time and energy to nurturing my precious children and supporting their endeavors.

     I consciously choose to abstain from engaging in sexual activities and avoid places that do not align with the practices of a virtuous woman. I firmly believe in upholding my dignity and self-respect, which is why I choose not to overly sexualize myself. This doesn't mean I am covered from head to toe, but rather, I refrain from flaunting my body. I am reserving these treasures for my future husband, as he is deserving of such reverence. When he appears in my life, he will recognize the value I hold within, treating me like a precious jewel, like the rarest of rubies.

I honor my faith and remain committed to leading a godly life by conducting myself in a way that is consistent with my beliefs. My choices represent my unshakeable dedication to honesty and virtue, and I am confident that a devoted and godly husband will value and recognize them.

A virtuous woman submits naturally. When it comes to the concept of submission, it's important to approach it with an open mind and a willingness to understand different perspectives. Submission in a marriage does not imply inferiority or suppression, but rather a mutual respect. It's about working together, making decisions together, and supporting his purpose.

As for letting your guard down, it can be a vulnerable process, but it's often necessary for personal growth and building deeper connections with your husband. It's important to establish trust and open communication within marriage, as it allows for honest and respectful dialogue.

I completely understand that relationships and personal callings can be complex topics. It's important to remember that everyone's journey is unique and there is no one-size-fits-all answer. While some individuals may feel a calling to be a wife, it's also essential to acknowledge that not all women are called to that role, and that's perfectly okay.

Remember, it's okay to have questions and uncertainties about these topics. Taking the time to explore your own desires, values, and goals is crucial. Ultimately, the most important thing is to be true to yourself and to find a path that brings you happiness and fulfillment. I am hoping that grabbing this book feels aligned with your spirit.

**Journal Prompt:** Being the Virtuous Woman I am Assigned to Be

Take a moment to reflect on your journey towards becoming a virtuous woman. Consider the qualities you admire in yourself and the areas you wish to improve.

- What does being a virtuous woman mean to you? How do you envision embodying these virtues in your daily life?

- Think about the qualities you possess that align with your vision of a virtuous woman. Write them down and celebrate them.

- Identify areas in which you would like to grow and improve. What steps can you take to cultivate these virtues within yourself?

- Do you understand the correlation between a virtuous woman and her submission to her husband's purpose?

- Consider the role of faith in your journey towards virtuousness. How has your relationship with God influenced your character development?

- Consider the mental and physical healing you will need to undergo following the emotional turmoil you go through by exposing your body and mind to someone who isn't your husband. Imagine doing it repeatedly until you are somewhat scarred by the time you meet your husband.

    - Food for thought: If you've previously dated someone who is inconsistent, abusive, or not good in bed there is a high probability that you may bring these preconceived notions to your husband.

*Journal here*

**Prayer prompt:** Being the Virtuous Woman I am Assigned to Be

Dear Heavenly Father,

    I come before You today, not only seeking to become a virtuous woman, but also to find a faithful man who walks according to your will. Help me discern the qualities of a man who aligns with your values, one who will support and uplift me on this journey.

    Grant me the wisdom to recognize a man who loves You above all things, who seeks to honor and serve You in every aspect of his life. May he be a man of integrity, displaying honesty, humility, and kindness in his actions and words.

    Lord, teach me the importance of submission within a loving and respectful relationship. Help me to understand that submission is not about inferiority, but about embracing the beautiful dance of marriage and mutual respect. Guide me as a virtuous woman while I await a man who finds me, cherishes me, and values my thoughts, desires, and dreams.

    As I pray for a faithful man, may I also cultivate a spirit of faithfulness within myself. Strengthen my commitment to You, Lord, and help me remain steadfast in my faith, regardless of the challenges I may face.

    Grant me the grace to submit, not only to a faithful man, but also to your divine will. Help me surrender my own desires and trust in your perfect plan for my life. May my submission be an act of love and trust, knowing that You have ordained my steps as a virtuous woman and have my best interests at heart.

    Lord, I pray for the wisdom to discern the balance between submission and maintaining my own identity. Help me to find strength in vulnerability and to express my needs and desires with grace and clarity.

Thank You for being a loving God who desires the best for me. Guide my steps, dear Lord, as I strive to become a virtuous woman who has a faithful man who will walk beside me on this journey.

In Jesus' name, I pray,

Amen.

Remember, that as you seek a faithful man, trust in God's timing and plan. Focus on becoming the best version of yourself, and in due time, the right person will come into your life. Trust in God's guidance and surrender to His will, knowing that He has a beautiful plan for you.

*My Prayer....*

# Day 23: Mothering My Children

**Scripture:** "Train up a child in the way he should go; even when he is old, he will not depart from it." - Proverbs 22:6

Proverbs 22:6 emphasizes the importance of nurturing and teaching children in a way that aligns with their unique qualities and strengths. By making deliberate choices to shield your children from negative influences and prioritize their well-being, you are actively training them to become strong, virtuous individuals who will carry those values into their future relationships and marriages. Your dedication to their spiritual growth and your reliance on prayer and guidance from God exemplify the love and commitment of a devoted mother.

As I write this, it's bittersweet because my daughter starts sixth grade next week and my son started his senior year two days ago. I've been doing this motherhood thing by myself for 10 years and I felt the need to write this for the mothers. That's why instead of doing a 30-day journal, I did a 31- day because I feel it's appropriate to speak to mothers and encourage them to grab this book as we can still be called to be a wife as well. Even if you aren't a mother, I still encourage you to read this chapter because it may give you insight into women in your family. Perhaps, it may even provide words or prayers for them. If you plan on being a mother, this is a good read for you too.

I always tell people that I'm definitely imperfect and weird, and those are my favorite qualities about myself. It makes me feel anchored. My children are my most prized gifts. With a failed marriage under my belt, I knew I owed it to them to make decisions for the greater good of us all. I have never allowed them to meet men that I've talked to, and I've never played house. When I say, "played house," I mean that I *don't allow* and *never have allowed* men to come to my place. This is my children's place of peace, so I will not have the energy and spirits of a man who is not my husband into their sacred space. This took discipline, and many would say sacrifice, but for me, it allowed growth and preservation. When I say preservation, I mean that my kids have always allowed me to respect myself because I wanted them to see me in an honest and vulnerable light. They understand that I'm human, but they also honor me by understanding that I have the ability to resist raggedy temptation on their behalf.

    Things that keep me grounded through motherhood include prayer, good friends, and my parents. I believe that one day I will be married to an amazing man of God. I don't want to expose my children's spirit to a man that is ill-qualified to be in their presence. I always told my son that I was single because I would never bring a man around that I couldn't look at and say, "I'm okay with you being just like him." Children are sponges. Most of the time, they are products of their environment, so I make sure I don't expose them to everything and everyone. I guide their hearts and minds while understanding that there are some things they have to experience, but a random man is not one of them. As you read this, I want you to give yourself grace and also use your kids as your secret weapon and your superpower. As mentioned previously, I got 3 of my 5 degrees as a single mother, and that's due to my kids and God.

    As I look at the humans that God assigned to me and entrusted me with, I feel emotional because they are amazing people. They will be great spouses one day. Listen, my kids lead me in prayer and talk to me about God. When I think of this, I know that it's God's grace that has kept and empowered me to make decisions that protect them and help them become great beings. They keep me grounded in God!

**Journal Prompt:** Mothering My Children

Reflect on your journey as a God-fearing mother and the ways in which you have demonstrated courage, communication, patience, and the recognition of your children as your superpower.

- Consider how you have taught your children about God and shown up for them.

Explore the strength you possess to keep them safe and shield them from harm or exposure to negative influences.

- Even if you aren't a mother, but desire to be one day, write about the ways in which you cover their lives with love and protection.

*Journal here*

**Prayer Prompt:** Mothering My Children

Dear Heavenly Father,

  Thank You for entrusting me with the precious gift of motherhood. I am grateful for the opportunity to raise my children in your ways and to guide them towards becoming strong, virtuous individuals. I humbly come before You today, seeking your guidance and strength as I reflect on my journey as a God-fearing mother.
  Lord, grant me the courage to make deliberate choices that shield my children from negative influences and prioritize their well-being. Help me to recognize their unique qualities and strengths. Guide me in nurturing them in a way that aligns with your will. Give me the wisdom to make decisions for the greater good of my family, even when it may require sacrifice.
  I pray for the strength to keep my children safe and protected, both physically and spiritually. Help me to shield them from harm and grant me discernment to recognize and avoid harmful situations. Give me the patience to navigate the challenges of parenting and to nurture their growth with love and understanding.
  Lord, I am grateful for the power of prayer and the guidance it brings. Help me to lead my children in prayer and teach them about your love and faithfulness. May our conversations be filled with open lines of communication, where we can discuss matters of the heart and seek your guidance together.
  Thank You, Lord, for the support of good friends and family who walk this journey with me. I pray that You continue to surround me with a community that uplifts and strengthens me as a mother. As I pray for a future partner in marriage, help me to attract a man of God who will be a positive influence in the lives of my children.

Father, I am in awe of the amazing individuals my children are becoming. I pray that You continue to guide and protect them, and that they may grow to be great spouses one day. Thank You for the privilege of being their mother and for the grace that has kept me and empowered me to make decisions that protect them.

In your holy name, I pray.

Amen.

## *My Prayer....*

# Day 24: Biological Clock

**Scripture:** "He has made everything beautiful in its time." - Ecclesiastes 3:11

This reminds us that God's timing is perfect and that we should trust in His plan for our lives. It is important to prioritize our spiritual hygiene and trust that God will provide according to His timing, rather than succumbing to societal pressures or feeling rushed into making decisions about marriage or starting a family. Remember, it is never too late for love, a child, or a husband if it aligns with God's will for your life. For complete wellbeing and to live in accordance with God's plan for your life, it is essential to take care of your physical, mental, and spiritual well-being, including maintaining womb health.

This is personal to me because I have personally witnessed conversations about the biological clock, such as "When are you getting married?" or "Are you dating? Time is running out." These questions are often posed to women in today's society and even in the past. However, I've come to realize that everything is in God's timing. If you have great spiritual hygiene, anything can happen. When faced with questions about our biological clock, please consider that God is great, and anything can happen through Him.

For example, my mom had me at the age of 19 and decided to get her tubes tied. Later, she got married again and wanted to conceive. However, they were only able to salvage one tube. Despite trying various treatments like artificial insemination and in-vitro, nothing happened. They then opted for adoption and now I have the most amazing little brother in the world. After his adoption was finalized, when I was 17, my mom found out she was pregnant. Now, I have a little sister who is one of my best friends. I always joke with her that I'm old enough to be her mother, literally.

The point I want to make is that you shouldn't let anyone dictate your time. It's never too late for love, a child, or a husband if that's what a child of God wants. I strongly advocate for prioritizing womb health and avoiding engaging in energetic exchanges with people whom you do not wish to marry. This is because such interactions can have a significant impact on both your physical and emotional well-being.

**Journal Prompt:** Biological Clock

Reflect on your own experiences and beliefs about the concept of the biological clock and God's timing.

- How have societal pressures or expectations influenced your thoughts and decisions regarding marriage and starting a family?

- How can you prioritize your spiritual hygiene and trust in God's plan for your life when faced with questions or doubts about your own timeline?

Consider any steps you can take to prioritize your physical and emotional well-being, including maintaining womb health and being intentional about the energetic exchanges you engage in.

*Journal here*

**Prayer Prompt:** Biological Clock

Dear Heavenly Father,

  Thank You for your perfect timing and the beauty of your plan for our lives. Help us to trust in your timing and not be swayed by societal pressures or expectations regarding marriage and starting a family. Remind us that it is never too late for love, a child, or a husband if it aligns with your will for our lives.
  Guide us in prioritizing our spiritual hygiene and seeking your wisdom and guidance in all aspects of our lives, relationships, and family planning. Help us protect our womb health and be intentional in our energetic exchanges to ensure we can take care of our physical and emotional well-being.
  Give us strength and confidence to stand firm in our convictions and make choices that align with your plan for our lives, even when faced with questions or doubts about our own timeline. Help us to remember that You are great, and anything can happen through You.
  We surrender our desires and plans to You, knowing that your timing is perfect. Help us to find peace and contentment in your will for our lives, trusting that You will provide for us according to your timing. May we always seek your guidance and trust in your plan.

  In Jesus' name, I pray.

Amen.

*My Prayer....*

# Day 25: Waiting and Fasting

**Scripture:** "Flee from sexual immorality. Every other sin a person commits is outside the body, but the sexually immoral person sins against his own body. Or do you not know that your body is a temple of the Holy Spirit within you, whom you have from God? You are not your own, for you were bought at a price. So, glorify God in your body." - 1 Corinthians 6:18-20

This scripture emphasizes the importance of avoiding sexual immorality and recognizing that our bodies are temples of the Holy Spirit. It reminds us that we are not our own, but rather, we belong to God. We should honor Him with our bodies. This aligns with the idea of cherishing sex as a sacred and meaningful act, rather than treating it as a casual or recreational activity.

Waiting and fasting can indeed be beneficial in preparing ourselves for a meaningful and fulfilling connection with our future partner. We create more cohesive thoughts while fasting. The true meaning of sex has been lost in today's world. However, we must remember that this powerful and energetic exchange between a man and a woman is a sacred and safe space for communication. It is a heavenly realm where there is no sin or judgment, allowing us to deeply connect with our partner as intended by God. Sadly, in today's society, sex is often not cherished as such and has become a mere recreational activity for many.

When I embarked on my own journey, I knew I had to approach it differently. I came to understand that celibacy refines our hearts and sharpens our minds. It wasn't just about abstaining from sexual activity; I also realized that engaging in masturbation, whether with or without pornography, was taking away from the potential experiences with my future spouse. I am far from perfect, and I would never claim to be, as I have had moments of faltering. However, I have come to understand the power of fasting and embracing the wait.

Waiting patiently allows us to truly appreciate the beauty and sanctity of the intimate connection we will have with our future partner. Through this wait, our hearts and minds are prepared for a profound and fulfilling experience.

Fasting, in addition to providing physical benefits such as detoxification and increased energy levels, can also offer mental clarity and spiritual connection. During fasting, we give our bodies and minds a break from the consumption of food, allowing us to focus our energy and attention on prayer, introspection, and self-reflection. It creates a space for increased mental clarity and a deeper sense of awareness, enabling us to strengthen our connection with our inner selves and with a higher power. Fasting instills discipline and self-control, both essential qualities when approaching sex with respect and mindfulness.

By practicing self-discipline through fasting, we develop the ability to make conscious and intentional choices, including those related to our sexual experiences. Incorporating fasting into our lives enhances our overall well-being and allows us to approach sex with a deeper sense of respect, mindfulness, and godliness.

So, let us remember the true meaning and significance of sex and approach it with patience, waiting for the right time and person, and utilizing fasting as a tool for mental clarity and spiritual connection. By doing so, we can create a foundation for a profound and fulfilling intimate connection with our future husband.

**Journal Prompt:** Waiting and Fasting

Reflect on any challenges or fears you might have regarding fasting.

- How do you currently view fasting? What are your thoughts and beliefs about its effectiveness in different areas of your life, including work, relationships, and personal growth? Consider the benefits of fasting mentioned, such as mental clarity, spiritual connection, patience, and an open mind. How do you think these qualities can positively influence your work, relationships, and personal growth? Are there specific areas where you feel these benefits would be particularly valuable?

- Have you ever incorporated fasting into your routine? If so, what was your experience like? How did it impact your mindset, discipline, and overall well-being?

- Are there any misconceptions or doubts that you need to address? How can you overcome these obstacles to fully embrace the potential benefits of fasting in your life?

- How can you ensure that fasting becomes a meaningful and intentional part of your journey?

*Journal here*

**Prayer Prompt:** Waiting and Fasting

Dear Heavenly Father,

    I come before You today with a humble heart, seeking guidance and wisdom in matters of sex, relationships, and personal growth. I acknowledge that You have created fasting as a powerful tool for spiritual discipline and preparation.

    Father, I confess that sometimes I underestimate the power of fasting in all aspects of my life. Help me to recognize that fasting is not only beneficial for abstaining from sex but also for cultivating patience, preparing for work, and approaching life with an open mind. Grant me the understanding that fasting can bring about a deeper connection with You and a heightened sense of self-awareness.

    During my times of fasting, I ask for your guidance and strength. May my fasts be moments of surrender, where I lay down my own desires and fully rely on your provision and direction. Help me to approach my work with diligence, perseverance, and a willingness to learn. May my fasting be a reminder to be patient and trust in your perfect timing in all areas of my life.

    Father, I surrender my impatience and the rush to fulfill my own desires. Fill me with a spirit of contentment and trust, knowing that You hold my future in your hands. Help me to use the time of fasting to cultivate patience, gratitude, and a deeper reliance on You.

    I thank You, Lord, for the gift of fasting and its transformative power. I trust in your perfect plan for my life. I know that through fasting, I can align my heart and mind with your will.

    In Jesus' name, I pray.

    Amen.

*My Prayer....*

# Day 26: Reflections of Love

**Scripture:** "Be devoted to one another in love. Honor one another above yourselves." - Romans 12:10

This scripture calls us to prioritize and honor one another in our relationships. It encourages us to be devoted to one another through love by placing the needs and well-being of others before our own. It teaches us to value and respect each other through cultivating a culture of love and mutual care.

As I reflect on the loving relationships that I have been fortunate enough to witness throughout my life, my first memory is of my grandmother and grandfather. He loved that woman. It was the first loving relationship I ever saw. To this day, I admire the way he loved her. I remember him always making her a priority, being attentive to her needs, praying over their home, working hard to make her happy, and being a provider for the home. I also remember the heartbreak when she passed away. Watching him grieve made me wonder if he would ever be able to move on. Surprisingly, he did, perhaps a little too quickly, according to some of his children, including my mother. She was deeply upset, saying, "Oh my goodness, my mom's grave doesn't even have grass over it yet, and he's already married!" I consoled her but now as an adult, I understand that the journey to finding love again can be different for everyone. In my grandfather's case, he got remarried to his high school sweetheart. Their engagement was intentionally short, as they believed in living a Christlike life. My mother and the rest of the family genuinely love his current wife, but it was our love for him that helped us accept, respect, and understand his choices. It's worth mentioning that he is a pastor and a man of God. His close relationship with God guided him to make the decisions he did, not our judgment. As a mature woman with more clarity and a stronger connection to God, I understand why he moved so fast. His prayer life and deep spiritual connection led him to know that she was meant to be his wife. They have now been happily married for 20+ years.

    The next relationship I witnessed firsthand was between my mother and my bonus dad. They started dating when I was five years old and by the time, I was seven, they were already married. When my mother began dating my bonus dad, he was only 19 years old, but their love has stood the test of time. Their relationship is truly beautiful to me because I have had the privilege of watching them grow from teenagers to mature adults. They may not be perfect, but they understand the importance of fulfilling their God-given roles in love and marriage. I pray that I find a partner who loves me as deeply as my grandfather and bonus dad love their wives. More importantly, I pray that I become a reflection of love for future generations to come.

**Journal Prompt:** Reflections of Love

Reflect on the loving relationships you have witnessed in your life and write about the lessons you have learned from them.

- o How have these relationships shaped your understanding of love? How do you hope to emulate and cultivate love in your own relationships?

- o If you have not witnessed a reflection of love firsthand, then write down ways to cultivate it.

- o Consider the qualities of patience, kindness, selflessness, and devotion mentioned in the scriptures discussed earlier. How can you incorporate these qualities into your interactions with others?

*Journal here*

**Prayer Prompt:** Reflections of Love

Dear Heavenly Father,

    Thank You for the loving relationships that I have witnessed in my life. I am grateful for the example of love and devotion that my grandmother and grandfather showed me. Their relationship has shaped my understanding of love and has inspired me to desire a similar kind of love in my own life.

    Lord, I pray that You guide me in cultivating love in my own relationships, especially in my future marriage. Help me to prioritize and honor my husband above myself, just as Romans 12:10 teaches. Grant me the qualities of patience, kindness, selflessness, and devotion, so that I may reflect your love to him.

    I pray specifically for my future husband. Lord, I ask that You bring the right man into my life, someone who loves You deeply and will love me unconditionally. Help me to recognize and appreciate the qualities that reflect your love in him. May he be a man who understands the importance of fulfilling his role as a husband and is committed to our marriage.

    As I wait for my future husband, I trust in your timing and your plan for my life. Help me to continue growing in my relationship with You, so that I may become a reflection of love for future generations. May my actions and words demonstrate the love and care that You have shown me.

    In Jesus' name, I pray.

    Amen.

*My Prayer....*

*Part Three: I's almost married now!*

*"To maintain the energetic frequency (posture) of him finding you, make sure to prepare yourself in the same way as you did before. Wake up each day with the intention to choose one another. This daily commitment will help strengthen your connection."*
~ *Dr. Dawn*

# Day 27: Order and Submission

**Scripture:** "Wives, submit yourselves to your own husbands as you do to the Lord. For the husband is the head of the wife as Christ is the head of the church, His body, of which He is the Savior. Now as the church submits to Christ, so also wives should submit to their husbands in everything."- Ephesians 5:22-24

This scripture emphasizes the importance of submission in marriage, comparing it to the submission of the church to Christ. It highlights the role of the husband as the head of the household and the responsibility of wives to submit to their husbands. Understanding the importance of order and submission in our roles as women is crucial. It is important to note that submission is not meant to be oppressive or demeaning, but rather a reflection of the order and structure that God has designed for marriage.

As the Bible says, finding a man who is in order, loves God, and seeks a virtuous woman is a blessing. As women, we are meant to be the helpmate to our husbands.

When getting to know a man, it is essential to inquire about his purpose and his relationship with God. If he lacks a clear understanding or knowledge of these aspects, he may not be the right match for you. It is important to be with someone who values delayed gratification, fasting, and prayer. Submission is submitting to a mission meaning the man has a clear purpose.

The idea of submission may be challenging for modern women due to advancements in women's rights, education, and access to power, it is important to reframe our thinking.

In light of advancements in women's rights, education, and opportunities for empowerment, it becomes imperative to redefine our understanding of submission in a way that aligns with the contemporary perspectives of women. When there is order in a relationship, the ability to submit and support our husband with their purpose flows naturally.

Submitting does not mean sacrificing our individuality, work, or education. On the contrary, our accomplishments and education contribute to our mission and enable us to better serve our husbands' purposes. Trust that God has guided us on our path to support and uplift our husbands. Remember, fulfilling our roles takes time and requires patience, trust, and a commitment to abstaining from sex until marriage.

Embrace the concepts of order and submission while maintaining your individuality and achievements. Pray for a man who knows God, has a strong foundation, and a relationship with Him. This will help create a harmonious marriage that allows both partners to fulfill their purposes. Trust in God's guidance and believe that you are on the right path to assist and uplift your husband and family. This ultimately fills both parties' cups and utilizes both of your gifts to accomplish the mission.

Lastly, the road to marriage should not be unnecessarily long. Take the time to get to know each other (court), pray together, and continue dating even after getting married.

**Journal Prompt:** Order and Submission

Reflect on your understanding of order and submission in your role as a woman.

- How do you feel about the idea of submitting to and supporting your husbands' purpose?

- How do you balance maintaining your individuality and achievements while embracing these concepts?

Write about any challenges or concerns you may have in regard to the road to marriage and how you envision navigating them.

*Journal here*

**Prayer Prompt:** Order and Submission

Heavenly Father,

I come before You with a humble heart, seeking wisdom and guidance in understanding the concepts of order and submission in my role as a woman. Help me to embrace these ideas with a renewed perspective, knowing that they do not diminish my individuality, work, or education, but rather contribute to my mission and enable me to better serve my husband's purpose.

Lord, I pray for a husband who knows and loves You, someone who understands the importance of order and seeks to fulfill their purpose with your guidance. Grant me discernment in getting to know a man's heart, his purpose, and his relationship with You. If he lacks a clear understanding or knowledge of these aspects, may I have the strength to recognize that he may not be the right match for me.

Lord, in a culture that prioritizes female empowerment, education, and accessibility to positions of authority, I recognize the difficulties that may come with embracing submission.

Help me to reframe my thinking and trust that when there is order in a relationship, the ability to submit and support my partner comes innately. Grant me the wisdom to balance maintaining my individuality and achievements while embracing the concept of submission.

Father, I commit myself to patience, trust, and a commitment to abstaining from sex until marriage as I navigate the road to marriage. Guide my future husband and I as we take the time to know each other, pray together, and continue dating even after getting married.

Lord, I surrender my concerns and challenges to You. I trust in your guidance and believe that You have led me on the right path to assist and uplift my partner and family. Help me to stay rooted in your word and rely on your strength as I navigate any obstacles that may come my way.

Thank you, Lord, for your love and guidance. I surrender my desires and intentions to You, knowing that You have a perfect plan for my life.

In Jesus' name, I pray.

Amen.

*My Prayer....*

# Day 28: Getting to the Aisle.

**Scripture:** "Two are better than one, because they have a good return for their labor: If either of them falls down, one can help the other up. But pity anyone who falls and has no one to help them up. Also, if two lie down together, they will keep warm. But how can one keep warm alone? Though one may be overpowered, two can defend themselves. A cord of three strands is not quickly broken."
- Ecclesiastes 4:9-12

This passage emphasizes the importance of having a supportive and loving partner in life. It suggests that a strong relationship can provide comfort, protection, and mutual assistance.

Let's be honest with ourselves: the displays that we have seen leading up to the aisle have shown toxicity, women having to stick by men who cheat, dealing with baby mama drama, verbal abuse, and trauma. However, this is simply not true. It is not true that the more we are put through, the more worthy we are of being someone's wife. Let's debunk that concept right now. Once your future husband finds you, it should be clear that you are not the one finding him. He should not be interested in going on lots of dates. Instead, you should be focusing on courting each other.

Courting is characterized by a focus on getting to know each other on a deeper level, with the intention of determining compatibility for marriage. It typically involves spending time together in group settings or with chaperones, setting boundaries, and prioritizing emotional and spiritual connection over physical intimacy. So, when people say, "dating with purpose," they're actually referring to courting. However, courting doesn't consist of a lot of dates, as many of us may not have the willpower to resist the temptation that comes along with traditional dating.

Instead, courting can involve activities like Face Timing, phone calls, and group outings. It's important to know yourself and your own boundaries. If you know that you're potentially going to give in to temptation on a hiking trail or in a car, which may lead to a hotel room, then intimate settings may not be the best course of action for you. You must be in tune with yourself and your own limits.

The courting process shouldn't be drawn out for years until engagement. Instead, it could be a matter of months to a year before getting engaged. After engagement, the time between engagement and marriage should also be relatively short. This is because we understand that once you have connected mentally, the desire to connect physically naturally arises. By keeping this part of the relationship shorter, you and your partner can enjoy each other's company on a Godly level and be intimate.

We have seen relationships where couples date for eight years and are engaged for 10 years, only to wonder why divorce often follows shortly after marriage. This is because they have already experienced the dynamics of marriage during their extended dating and engagement period, which diminishes the value of the actual marriage.

Along with focusing on getting to know each other on a deeper level, praying together and establishing a relationship with Christ is a crucial aspect of courting. By praying together, you and your partner can seek guidance, strength, and wisdom from God as you navigate your relationship. It allows you to invite God into every aspect of your courtship, ensuring that your foundation is built on faith and shared values.

Establishing a relationship with Christ not only strengthens your individual faith but also strengthens the bond between you and your partner. By growing spiritually together, you can support and encourage each other's spiritual journey, deepening your connection on a soulful level. It allows you to align your values, beliefs, goals, and lay a solid foundation for a God-centered and fulfilling marriage.

Prayer and maintaining a relationship with Christ are not only important during the courting phase, but also throughout your entire marriage. Continuously seeking God's guidance, wisdom, and blessings will help you navigate the ups and downs of married life, keeping your bond strong and your love rooted in faith. So, in addition to courting, make sure to prioritize praying together and nurturing your relationship with Christ as you prepare for a lifelong commitment.

Remember, even after getting married, it's important to continue dating each other to keep the marriage fresh and to continue getting to know one another. As people we evolve, dating helps with that evolution. This will help to maintain a strong and fulfilling marriage.

**Journal Prompt:** Getting to the Aisle.

Reflect on your own boundaries and how they align with the concept of courting. Share your thoughts on the duration of the courting process and the time between engagement and marriage.

- What are your thoughts on the idea of getting to know someone on a deeper level before marriage?

- How do you feel about prioritizing emotional and spiritual connection over physical intimacy?

Finally, consider the importance of continuing to date and evolving together even after getting married.

- How do these ideas resonate with you and your own desires for a strong and fulfilling marriage?

*Journal here*

**Prayer Prompt:** Getting to the Aisle.

Dear Heavenly Father,

    I lift up my desire for a strong and fulfilling marriage to You. As I navigate the courting process, I pray that my future husband and I would prioritize growing together as a couple with Christ at the center of our relationship.
    Help us to establish a foundation of prayer and spiritual connection as we get to know each other on a deeper level. May our conversations be filled with your wisdom and guidance, and may we seek your will in all aspects of our relationship.
    I pray that You would bless our time together, whether it be through Face Timing, phone calls, or group outings. May these activities strengthen our bond and allow us to grow closer to You and to each other.
    Grant us the strength to remain faithful to You and to each other, even in times of temptation. Help us to set boundaries that honor You and protect our hearts and purity.
    In the courting process, I ask for your guidance and discernment. Show us if we are meant to journey towards marriage together, and if so, lead us towards that commitment with confidence and peace.
    As we move towards engagement and marriage, I pray for your timing and direction. May the time between engagement and marriage be filled with joy, preparation, and anticipation for the lifelong commitment we are making.
    Finally, I ask for your grace and wisdom as we continue to date and evolve together even after getting married. Help us to prioritize our relationship with You and with each other, always seeking to grow and deepen our love.

Thank You, Lord, for your presence in our lives and for the gift of marriage. May our relationship be a testament to your love and grace.

In Jesus' name,

Amen.

*My Prayer....*

# Day 29: A Prayer for The Wife I'm Called to Be

**Scripture:** "So do not fear, for I am with you; do not be dismayed, for I am your God. I will strengthen you and help you; I will uphold you with my righteous right hand." - Isaiah 41:10

    This scripture serves as a comforting reminder that God is always with us, offering His strength and support in times of fear and discouragement. It reassures us that we do not need to be afraid or dismayed because the Almighty God is our God and He promises to uphold us with His righteous right hand. This scripture encourages us to trust in God's presence and provision, knowing that He will empower us and assist us in every situation we face. It reminds me to rely on God's strength and not be overwhelmed by fear or worry. He is always there to support and guide me.

    As I pray for the wife I am called to be, it is important for me to remember to prioritize God and trust in His guidance. In times of insecurity, self-doubt, defeat, stress, or even when facing illness or death, I can always seek solace in God. Even if my mind becomes clouded, I can still communicate with Him. Even if I lose my voice, I can still connect with Him in my heart. I can always turn to Him, for He is the one who will support and guide me. I come to God equally when things are beautiful and full of sorrow. I acknowledge that it is just as important to express gratitude and seek guidance in moments of happiness as it is in times of struggle. Whether I am experiencing blessings, milestones, or achievements, I know that it is by God's grace that I am able to enjoy these moments. I offer my gratitude and acknowledge that He is the source of all goodness in my life. God has always been present in my life and it is crucial for me to never lose sight of that.

I always pray for my future marriage and for myself to become the wife that God has called me to be, but also the wife that my husband needs me to be. I understand that each marriage is unique. My husband may have specific needs and desires that I should strive to fulfill. I pray for wisdom, discernment, and the ability to understand his heart and support him in the best way possible.

I also pray for the strength to be a supportive and loving helpmate to my husband. I want to be there for him in times of joy, sorrow, success, and failure. I want to listen to him with an open heart, communicate honestly and openly, and always strive to honor God in my actions, words, and thoughts towards him.

In moments of conflict or difficulty, I seek God's guidance and ask for His wisdom to navigate through challenges. I recognize that my own desires and emotions should not drive my actions, but rather I should rely on God's everlasting love and faithfulness to guide me in being the wife my husband needs.

I also take my role as a wife seriously and understand that I should never be too arrogant to drop down on my knees or my face and pray if the marriage is not going well. I recognize that there will be ups and downs in our relationship. When it is my turn to carry the weight, I strive to do it with grace and peace. I believe in finding a balance where we can always include each other in our lives. I am willing to hold my husband's hand and be the helpmate I am called to be.

**Journal Prompt:** A Prayer for The Wife I'm Called to Be

- How can you prioritize God and trust in His guidance in your role as a wife?

- How can you seek His wisdom in your marriage?

- What does it mean to you to be a supportive and loving helpmate to your husband?

Reflect on how you can fulfill this role with grace and peace, finding a balance where you can include each other in your lives.

*Journal here*

**Prayer Prompt:** A Prayer for The Wife I'm Called to Be

Dear Heavenly Father,

Thank You for the reminder in Isaiah 41:10 that we do not need to fear or be dismayed because You are always with us. You promise to strengthen, help, and to uphold us with your righteous right hand. Help me to hold onto this truth as I strive to be the wife You have called me to be.

Lord, I pray that I never lose sight of your presence in my life and in our marriage. When I face moments of insecurity, self-doubt, or stress, remind me to turn to You for solace and guidance. Help me to trust in your strength and not be overwhelmed by fear or worry. When I feel weak, empower me with your Spirit to be a supportive and loving helpmate to my husband.

In times of happiness and joy, I also ask for the awareness to express gratitude and seek your guidance. Help me to remember that all blessings and goodness comes from You and to always acknowledge your presence in our lives.

Lord, when our marriage faces challenges and difficulties, I pray that I approach them with humility and a desire to seek your wisdom. Grant me the grace to communicate openly and honestly with my husband, listening with open ears and a receptive heart. Help us to function from a space of the Holy spirit, relying on your guidance and strength, rather than being driven by our own fleshly desires.

Overall, I pray for the grace to fulfill my role as a wife with humility, love, and a deep trust in God's guidance. I believe that with His help, I can strive to be the wife that God has called me to be and the wife my husband needs in our journey of marriage.

Thank You, Lord, for the gift of marriage and for the role I have as a wife. May I always strive to honor You in my actions, words, and thoughts. Guide me each day to be the wife You desire me to be, leaning on your everlasting love and faithfulness.

In Jesus' name, I pray.

Amen.

*My Prayer....*

# Day 30: A Prayer for My Husband

**Scripture:** "Husbands, love your wives, just as Christ loved the church and gave Himself up for her." -Ephesians 5:25

As mentioned in the beginning of my book, this is not intended for non-believers or close-minded individuals. When I envision my husband, I associate him with peace, companionship, serenity, my edges, healthy eating, kindness, vulnerability, moments of tears, and warm weather. The embrace of his arms feels like dancing naked in the rain, accompanied by the thunderous sounds. I think of engaging in unprotected, holy sex, free from STDs, concerns about Plan B or pregnancy. It brings to mind the intimate act of making love while gospel music plays. This is grown woman, holy sex with my husband. It is blessed and leads to fruitful outcomes. It inspires thoughts of building an empire, earning money, spreading the gospel, and engaging in prayer. The essence of blessed sex is indescribable, amplifying, and safeguarding my life.

To support these thoughts, I wait and have faith that God will provide me with everlasting joy, which I will experience with my husband. Everlasting joy doesn't mean life will be without battles; it means that you'll face life's challenges, such as death, illness, rebellious kids, mental health issues, etc., but you'll have someone you can trust and depend on to face them together. This person is not just a best friend or lover; they are someone who is there for you even when you can't rely on yourself. They love you despite your shortcomings, your sexual performance, the size of your butt, or any physical changes that may occur due to breast cancer, alopecia, endometriosis, and other conditions. They love the core of your being, your spirit, and they are assigned to you.

     Now, because I have certifications and degrees that support this next portion, I'm going to speak to my women who have inner child trauma and trust issues because I've been there. You're probably wondering how you can trust someone to not give you an STD. People may think, "Oh no, I'm always going to protect myself. I'm not going to be stupid and allow somebody to have me thinking it's all good." At this point in the book, we should have prayed through some of those obstacles, but just in case we haven't, I want you to understand that if you've nurtured those pieces of yourself, healed your inner child, generational trauma, and perhaps even used the tool therapy, you will understand that just like you exist and are on your path, there's another person that God has aligned for you. They are listening, fasting, praying, and abstaining for you. That's what we call blind faith! Even with prayer, challenges may arise, but it's important to pray through them. Life is about embracing the layers and remaining faithful and true. It's through experiences that we grow and learn. Don't bank on perfection but do have faith. This act is called faith and surrendering.

**Journal Prompt:** A Prayer for My Husband

Take a moment to write down the qualities and values you want in your future husband. Reflect on how these qualities align with your own aspirations and dreams for a fulfilling and loving marriage.

- What steps can you take to prepare yourself for the journey of marriage and create a strong foundation for a blessed and fruitful union?

*Journal here*

**Prayer Prompt:** A Prayer for My Husband

Dear Heavenly Father,

I come to You today with gratitude, hope, seeking your blessings for my future husband. I pray that he not only loves You deeply, but also appreciates and values everything that we create together, whether it be our home, our family, or our shared dreams and endeavors.

Please, bless him with a heart that cherishes the beauty of our creations, recognizing the time, effort, and love we invest in them. Grant him the ability to appreciate the intricacies, details, the functionality and integrity of all that we build together.

Father, I also pray that he loves me and our children unconditionally, both as a unit and as individuals. May he understand the unique needs, desires, and dreams that each one of us possesses. Help him to navigate the challenges and joys of parenting. Lord, I understand that our marriage is a sacred bond, a covenant between ourselves and You. I pray that my future husband holds this truth close to his heart, honoring and respecting our marriage as a lifelong commitment. May he always affirm our union with wisdom, patience, and love.

It is not just a legal contract, but a spiritual one, rooted in love, trust, and devotion.

Grant him the strength and determination to stand by our side, through thick and thin, for better or worse, till death do us part. Help him to prioritize our family and our relationship, always striving to nurture and protect the love we share.

I trust in your divine plan, dear God, and I know that You have the perfect husband for me. As I wait for our paths to intersect, I pray that You mold my future husband into the man You desire him to be. Prepare his heart, mind, and soul for the incredible journey we will embark upon together.

Dear Lord, I humbly ask that You bless my future husband with the ability to pray and cover our family in your love and protection. Grant him the wisdom to seek your guidance and to intercede on behalf of our family in times of joy, sorrow, and uncertainty.

In moments when he feels weak or overwhelmed, I pray that he turns to You, Heavenly Father, knowing that he has a steadfast helper who is always there to assist him with all of his needs. Strengthen his faith and grant him the assurance that through You, he can find solace, strength, and courage to face any challenge that comes our way.

May God grant me the words to pray and intercede on behalf of my husband. May I be able to communicate with Him and pray for my husband during his moments of vulnerability and need. May my husband feel and understand that I have faith in him and our purpose.

Lord, I pray for my husband's spiritual growth. Help him to deepen his relationship with You and to seek your guidance in all areas of his life. Give him a hunger for your Word and a desire to live in accordance with your will. Strengthen his faith and help him to trust in your plans and purposes for our lives.

May he be a spiritual leader in our home, leading by example, and encouraging us to deepen our relationship with You. Help him to prioritize prayer by studying your Word, and seeking your will in all aspects of our lives.

Lord, I trust that You will provide a husband for me, who not only loves us, but also loves You wholeheartedly. I pray that our union will be a reflection of your love and grace and a testament to the power of faith and commitment.

Lord, I also pray that everything my future husband and I touch be fruitful. May our endeavors, whether it be our careers, our personal pursuits, or our endeavors in service to others, bear abundant blessings and bring glory to your name.

    I ask that You bless our union with prosperity, not only in material wealth, but also in spiritual growth and emotional well-being. May our love and commitment to one another serve as a strong foundation for our future generations, inspiring them to seek and embrace the sanctity of marriage.

    In your divine presence, we humbly come before You, seeking your blessings upon our sacred union. I pray for a truly enchanting and holy sex life with my beloved husband. May our intimate moments be touched by your grace, flowing with compassion, tenderness, and creating a beautiful exchange of love and pleasure. Illuminate our connection with vibrant colors and radiant light, transforming our bedroom into a safe and sacred space, where we can fully express our love for one another.

    With gratitude and trust, we surrender ourselves to your guidance, knowing that You will bless our union with unconditional love, holiness, and joy. Grant us the grace to navigate through the challenges that may arise in our journey together. Give us the grace to communicate effectively, to resolve conflicts with humility and forgiveness, and to always cherish and prioritize our relationship. Help us to communicate with love, respect, and understanding, so that our love becomes a shining example to our past and future generations. May our relationship reflect the beauty of your design for marriage and the sanctification that comes through it.

    Lord, I pray that our love serves as a testimony to others, showing them the value of marriage and the transformative power of your love. May our relationship be a beacon of hope and inspiration, pointing others towards the path of true love and commitment.

    Thank You, dear God, for the gift of love and the promise of my future spouse. I trust in your divine plan and surrender our desires for a blessed and fruitful union into your loving hands.

I thank You for the gift of his presence in my life and for the love and commitment he has shown me. I ask that You bless him abundantly and guide him in all aspects of his life.

Father, I pray that my husband would love me as Christ loves the church. Teach him to be selfless, compassionate, always seeking to serve, and support us in all we do.

Father, I ask for wisdom and discernment for my husband. Guide him in his decision-making and grant him clarity of mind. Help him to make choices that are pleasing to You and that align with your perfect will. Give him the courage to stand firm in his convictions and to lead our family with love and integrity.

Lord, I pray for my husband's physical and emotional well-being. Protect him from illness, injury, and grant him strength and vitality. Help him to find rest and rejuvenation in your presence. Heal any wounds or hurts he may carry and fill his heart with peace and joy.

Father, I pray for my husband's relationships with others. Help him to be a man of kindness and compassion, treating others with respect and love. Give him wisdom in his interactions with friends, family, and colleagues. May he be a source of encouragement and support to those around him.

Lord, I lift up my husband's dreams and aspirations to You. Help him to discover and pursue the passions and talents You have placed within him. Guide him in his career and give him success in his endeavors. May he find fulfillment and purpose in his work, using his gifts to bring glory to your name.

Father, I pray for our marriage. Help us to grow in love and unity each day. Lord, I trust in your perfect plan for my husband's life. I surrender him into your loving hands, knowing that You will guide and protect him.

Thank You, dear God, for hearing my prayer and for guiding my future husband's steps. I surrender our desires and dreams into your loving hands, knowing that You will bring them to fruition in your perfect timing.

In Jesus' name, I pray.

Amen.

May this prayer bring you comfort and hope as you entrust your desires and dreams to God. Remember to have faith and patience, knowing that His plans are greater than anything we can imagine.

*My Prayer....*

# Day 31: Covering Our Union Now and Forever

**Scripture:** "For our struggle is not against flesh and blood, but against the rulers, against the authorities, against the powers of this dark world and against the spiritual forces of evil in the heavenly realms." - Ephesians 6:12

This verse reminds us that there are spiritual battles happening around us, including attacks on our marriages. By recognizing this and turning to prayer, we can seek God's guidance, protection, and strength to overcome these challenges and protect our union.

Covering your union is a daily task and your life's work. You have to remember that the devil does not want to see a healthy union, so he's constantly going to be attacking your marriage. It is for the two of you to understand this concept and choose each other every day. To do this, you should wake up and pray, whether it be together or separately. Pray for your marriage and the children in that marriage. You should be praying with them and end the day with prayer. This is just the baseline; anything else you do is in addition.

Make sure that you are communicating and sharing your day with one another. Even when you're upset and irritated, make sure you're spending intimate time together. This looks like praying together, hugging, and transferring energy to charge one another. This is vital, like sealing a deal with a handshake. People say, "Don't go to bed mad," and that's cute, but don't go to bed without covering your union. It's essential to be mindful of the power of the Holy Spirit and communication. Your union is going to have to have the power to walk through pain and devastation together, so it must be covered by the blood of Jesus. Learn each other so deeply that, even without words, you know your partner's needs and desires, and when in doubt, pray it out. The same way you prayed to have a husband, to have children, to have a career, you have to apply that to your marriage. Multiple times a day, the enemy will attack everything from your finances to children and health. Things are going to happen. Prayer is prevention. Prayer is medicine. Prayer is God. Prayer is profound. It is required to protect your union.

**Journal Prompt:** Covering Our Union Now and Forever

- How do you envision navigating challenges, overcoming obstacles, and growing together spiritually?

- Consider the role of prayer in protecting and strengthening your future union. How can you incorporate daily prayer into your marriage to seek God's guidance, protection, and blessings?

Reflect on the power of prayer to shape and safeguard your future union.

- Write down specific prayers or intentions you have for your partnership.

- How will you commit to covering your future union in prayer starting now?

*Journal here*

**Prayer Prompt:** Covering Our Union Now and Forever

Dear Heavenly Father,

 Thank You for the gift of marriage and the desire You have placed in my heart for a future husband. I come before You today, acknowledging the spiritual battles that may surround my future union. I recognize that my struggle is not against flesh and blood, but against the rulers, authorities, and powers of this dark world. I find hope and comfort in knowing that through prayer, I can seek your guidance, protection, and strength to overcome these challenges.
 Lord, I commit to covering my future union in prayer. I understand that the enemy does not want to see a healthy and God-centered marriage, and he will try to attack and undermine this union. Help me to wake up each day and choose to pray, seeking your will and guidance in him finding me. May prayer be the foundation of communication, trust, and intimacy in my future marriage.
 Even in times of doubt or impatience, Lord, remind me to come before You in prayer, surrendering my desires and trusting in your perfect timing. Help me to embrace the power of prayer, knowing that it is not only a preventive measure, but also a source of healing, strength, and profound connection with You. Teach me to lean on You and to trust in your plans for my future.
 Father, I ask for your guidance and protection over my future husband. Lead him on a path of growth and spiritual maturity. Surround him with your love, protection, and prepare his heart for the commitment of marriage. Help him to recognize me and vice versa when the time is right and grant us the wisdom and discernment to build a strong and God-honoring relationship.
 Lord, I pray for the qualities and characteristics You desire in a future husband for me. May he be a man after

your own heart, filled with love, kindness, and integrity. Help him to prioritize his relationship with You above all else, seeking your guidance in every aspect of his life. Give him wisdom, strength, and a heart that desires to serve and honor You.

Father, I commit to covering my future union in prayer now and in the future. I trust that You have a perfect plan for my life and my future marriage. Help me to remain patient and faithful, knowing that your timing is always perfect. I surrender my desires and dreams to You, confident that You will guide the husband You have prepared for me to find me!

In Jesus' name, I pray.

Amen.

*My Prayer....*

# Postscript

"Houses and wealth are inherited from parents, but a prudent wife is from the Lord." - Proverbs 19:14

This verse emphasizes that a wise and suitable spouse is a gift from God. It reminds us that finding the right person is not solely dependent on our efforts, but ultimately comes from God's providence and guidance.

Dear future wife,

If you have taken this course seriously and have been adamant about journaling and doing your prayers, you are at a point where you have a great prayer life. You can see areas of your life where things have grown, and maybe some things have been out of whack or different. But in those moments, you were able to pray and transform through them because no new path is necessarily easy. You probably have a lot of questions, and hopefully, they were answered throughout the book. Remember love is a lifelong journey, not a goal. Love is an action word. I hope that by reading these chapters, you understand what your soul requires to attract a man of God and have him find you.

Please, remember that you can do many of these journal prompts over and over and even read your prayers, so you remember the foundation of your thoughts. You can actually go through the book a few times if needed to progress in your prayer life, as you will always need to be praying for all the moments in your life; including your marriage.

As a steadfast companion on your spiritual journey, I stand alongside you with unwavering support and encouragement. I want to address a topic that may be weighing heavily on your heart - the power of intercessory prayer and the impact it can have on our lives and the lives of others. Yes, prayers work, but sometimes God's answer is, "no or not right now."

When faced with challenges or uncertainty, we often turn to prayer as a source of strength and solace. You have a unique gift, a divine calling to intercede on behalf of others. Through your prayers, you have the ability to make a profound difference in their lives.

In this world where trials and tribulations abound, it is essential to remember the immense power of prayer. Your prayers have the potential to uplift, heal, and bring about transformation. I encourage you to embrace this role fully and wholeheartedly.

In addition to intercessory prayer, consider keeping a prayer journal as a means of deepening your connection with God. By documenting your prayers, experiences, and reflections, you can witness the ways in which God works in your life and the lives of those you pray for.

Being a Prayer Warrior means being vigilant and intentional. It means standing firm in your faith, even when faced with doubts or trials. Trust in God's perfect timing and trust in the power of your prayers.

As you continue on this prayerful journey, know that you are not alone. I am here praying for all the readers, offering support and encouragement. Together, let us embrace the calling to be Prayer Warriors, lifting others up in prayer, and witnessing the transformative power of God's grace.

With heartfelt prayers and unwavering support,

Dr. Dawn

# About the Author

I am the Director of Operations at a Trauma Center in Southern California with extensive experience as a healthcare director spanning over a decade. I have a diverse background in Mental Health Leadership, Men's Health and surgical centers. I have opened IOP/PHP programs and ASCs for companies across the world. I am also a Professor at a local college.

In my spare time, I offer Somatic therapy, Brainspotting therapy, Reiki, and sound bath meditation for my own clients. My ultimate goal is to assist with holistic healing in the BIPOC community. I believe that the sky is the limit when God is in it!

# References:

Chicago. hooks, bell, 1952-2021. All about Love : New Visions. New York :William Morrow, 2000.

Nelson, T. (2018). *NIV, The Woman's Study Bible, Hardcover, Full-Color: Receiving God's Truth for Balance, Hope, and Transformation.*

*The Hoodhealer* (By I. Cohen [The Hoodhealer]). (2019). [Video]. Instagram Live.

*Woman's New Kings James version* (3rd ed.). (2010). Life Pub Intl.

**Editor :** Avianna Velez
**Book Cover:** Avianna Velez
**Published by:** DrDawn.life Reads

Made in the USA
Columbia, SC
16 January 2024

8d6e9678-7902-49ca-86c5-5d1a4660eadeR01